Values Added

Making Ethical Decisions in the
Financial Marketplace

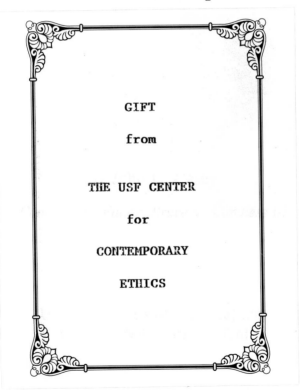

Copyright © 1997 by
University Press of America,® Inc.
4720 Boston Way
Lanham, Maryland 20706

3 Henrietta Street
London, WC2E 8LU England

Library of Congress Cataloging-in-Publication Data

Casey, John L.
Values added : making ethical decisions in the financial marketplace /
by John L. Casey ; contributing editor, Bruce McCandless III.
p.   cm.
Includes bibliographical references
1. Finance--Moral and ethical aspects--United States. I. McCandless,
Bruce, III. II. Title.
HG181.C375 1996   174'.9332--dc21   96-46347 CIP

ISBN 0-7618-0609-1 (cloth: alk. ppr.)
ISBN 0-7618-0610-5 (pbk: alk. ppr.)

Contents

Acknowledgments

Dolores Prehle has for years helped me to keep my life in order, an essential function particularly during major projects such as producing *Values Added*. When I told her I was pecking away at my computer keyboard, trying to identify the many people who have inspired me and assisted on the project over the past three years, Dolores just laughed. She added, "You'll need a second book to include them all."

True enough. But as no such volume would be likely to catch the fancy of readers, I'll have to surf this shortened list.

Values Added is dedicated to:

George S. Johnston. George, who died recently, was for 30 years my friend and teacher at Scudder, Stevens & Clark. He was a special hero who never ceased to ask the ethical question, "But is it good for the clients?"

The Moorhead Kennedy Group. Moorhead Kennedy, Brenda Repland, and Martha Keys have been pioneers in the field of alternative communication, including role-playing simulations designed to teach ethics through participation.

The Center for Business Ethics at Bentley College. Michael Hoffman, Judy Kamm, and Edward Petry, with their extended family of faculty and fellows, as well as members of other departments, like Len Rosenthal, have welcomed me in their discussions, their debates — even their classrooms.

The Program in Ethics and the Professions at Harvard University. Directed by Dennis Thompson, this important enterprise welcomes and fosters both the practical input of managers like me and some of the field's most advanced academic research.

Many thanks go to my old friends at Scudder. In addition to instruction in derivatives from Gary Johnson, I received help on the book's title from Janice Battikha and Laury Kassell; on the European perspective on business ethics from Richard Lewy in London; on corporate social responsibility issues from Melissa Kirby; and on general focus from Dennis Cronin and Alan Blackmer.

At Harvard, I am indebted to Solomon Benatar, M.D., Paula Duffy, Carol Franco, Mary Gentile, and Marjorie Williams. Roger Cheever and Janet Averill introduced me to the Program in Ethics and the Professions. Joseph Badaracco, Jr. illuminated the predacious environment many of our young managers are dropped into, an unpleasant fact that refocused the book. From Richard Pittblado I received intelligent and detailed comments.

Steve Brenner and Judge Diarmuid O'Scannlain gave me the chance to test some of the ideas and techniques in *Values Added* at Portland State University.

Encouragement and exhortation have flowed from Roger Boisjoly, James Connor, S.J., Horace Deets, Ron Green, Barbara Gregorovich, John Langan, S.J., Paul Lansing, Don McCabe, Laura Nash, Chuck Powers, Barbara Ley Toffler, and Patricia Werhane. I received valuable suggestions on the text from Jan Allison, Jim Ballentine, Meredith Brown, Msgr. Harry Byrne, Brett Carlson, Ambrose Carr, Patricia Fuller, George Gowen, Jeff Kaplan, Bob Kaufmann, Robert Lear, Arthur Levitt, Alfred Malabre, Ted Necarsulmer, Ted Niedermayer, Suzie Peck, Myles Whalen, Kathy Whitbeck, and Vincent Yeh.

The people and institutions depicted in *Values Added* are entirely fictional. No resemblance to actual people or institutions is intended or endorsed.

Introduction

Values Added is a re-imagining of my previous book, *Ethics in the Financial Marketplace*, which has been a staple in Wall Street quarters for several years. An early version of the *EFMP* manuscript won the Leubsdorf Award from the Financial Analysts Research Federation in 1984. The finished product became required reading for qualifying as a Chartered Financial Analyst, and turned up in such various places as Sophia University in Tokyo and the Salomon Brothers trading desk in New York.

Now, with the invaluable assistance of Bruce McCandless III, I have built into this new work many of the countless suggestions and comments I've received over the years from my readers, co-panelists, and students. I hope that in *Values Added* I have communicated a set of steps that will help financial professionals to make responsible decisions in an ever more global, complex, and volatile financial environment.

John L. Casey

Acknowledgments

On the production side, my thanks go to Chris Schenk and Bill Walsh; to Ron Duska and *Business Ethics* magazine; to my literary agent, John Ware; to typesetter extraordinaire Dorothy Albritton; and especially to Nancy Ulrich and Helen Hudson at the University Press of America.

Every one of the people above, and many more besides, helped shape *Values Added*. Much of the credit is theirs. All the mistakes are still mine.

Finally, my thanks for permission to reprint previously published material from:

Random House, Inc., publisher of *Bombadiers*, by Po Bronson. Copyright 1995 by Po Bronson.

Simon & Schuster, publisher of *Catch-22*, by Joseph Heller. Copyright 1955, 1961 by Joseph Heller. Copyright renewed 1989 by Joseph Heller.

Introduction

Money often costs too much.

Ralph Waldo Emerson

Chapter 1

Seven Easy Pieces:
A Checklist for Ethical Action

What matters most isn't my beliefs. It's yours.

This book sets out seven steps intended to help financial professionals make job-related decisions that reflect their personal beliefs. It's a guide to traveling the places where character meets cash. It's a book, that is, about ethics.

Maybe you wonder, *Why should I bother to read about ethics?* After all, most of us in finance have plenty to do already. But there are several good reasons.

Self

First, acting ethically has significant personal benefits. As the following chapters demonstrate, a concern for fairness can be just as important to making sound professional decisions as powerful microprocessors and the latest forecasting software. Proceeding deliberately, with respect for your own beliefs and attention to the consequences of your actions, can help you avoid some very large traps.

The Profession

Second, responsible decisions benefit the financial industry in general. It's hard to say when Wall Street conquered the world. What's clear is that it did. Today the Russians swap common stocks of their own. Former followers of Marx and Mao now actively seek outside investment. Officially or not, every major nation recognizes the importance of healthy capital markets in the development of a sturdy economy. In short, the world wants money. Wall Street money. And the ability to make its own.

Meanwhile, Americans are finally overcoming the collective trauma of the Great Depression. The Glass-Steagall Act's statutory wall between the worlds of commercial and investment banking is slowly crumbling. Congress has recently cut back on both prospectus disclosure requirements and the ability of the plaintiffs' bar to bring frivolous securities fraud suits. In these respects, the future looks a lot like many financial professionals have always hoped. But deregulation didn't work so well when it was applied to the savings & loan industry. So how will loosening the statutory straps affect money management, investment banking, and stock brokerage?

That's up to us. Now more than ever, we who work on Wall Street—whether in New York or Dallas, Denver or L.A.—have to know how to govern ourselves. It's partly a matter of moment. Through stocks and bonds, mutual funds and pension plans, we now control unprecedented amounts of invested money. American financial institutions are in turn pumping that money into fledgling industries all over the world, from Tashkent to Thailand, from Mexico to Malaysia. We need to act responsibly now not only because we're being given a second chance to do so, but also because the consequences of our failure could be disastrous.

Society

Finally, we ought to act responsibly in our business for the same reason everyone else should in theirs. The alternative to individual ethics is *legislated* ethics—rules, rules, and more rules. Of course we need laws. But laws alone are a poor substitute for morality. The greatest blessing of living in a free society is that we have the ability to steer ourselves. Once we give up that ability, that privilege, we risk losing sight of the ethical spirit the law attempts to codify. Lose that ethical spirit and the law becomes a cage. We'll do, as so many others have done in this century, just what we're told to do. The world can no longer afford that kind of obedience.

Defining "Ethics"

Reasonable people may differ on questions of what is ethical in a given situation. What we all might agree on, however, is a basic definition of "ethics" itself. "Ethics" is about how we translate our biggest beliefs—faith in God, self-respect, pride in family or flag—into our treatment of other people. Anchored in such ideas, ethical conduct tends to be conduct that is not wholly self-serving. It assumes that the individual is part of a larger enterprise, and urges him to act so that the larger enterprise is helped, or at least not hindered, by his actions.

Consider two figures from the crowded pantheon of popular culture. Gordon Gekko, the knife-like M&A man who dominates Oliver Stone's subtle-as-a-sledgehammer movie *Wall Street*, is not an ethical guy. He acts purely from self-interest. (Whether one can have an ethic *of* self-interest, a sort of creed of greed, is a mildly interesting but not very fruitful line of discussion. Certainly one could rationalize acting out of unreflective self-interest on the ground that Adam Smith's hidden hand or the clever counterweights of a clockmaker God could make everything come out all right in the end. But wouldn't that be the same as acting without any ethics at all?)

Gekko's protege, and ultimately his antagonist, is a starstruck young securities trader who reveals himself to be at least vestigially ethical. Bud Fox realizes that his stock-strafing games are hurting other people. He also sees that, because this is true, he's damaging a larger enterprise—call it "the American economy," though it could just as easily be labeled "America itself," "the American family," or "life on Earth"—by doing so. Then he tries to salvage himself. And okay, yeah, the attempt involves an ethically suspect bit of covert tape recording. *So what?* This is Hollywood, where any means is justified by a satisfying end. And the point, as most of us knew before we entered the octoplex in the first place, is that a life devoted solely to self creates a self not worth the devotion.

The Checklist

Advanced academic research and plain old common sense both suggest that our moral character starts to take shape early in life, just around the time we stop drooling. We learn right and wrong from our folks. We learn in our churches, and temples, and synagogues. We learn from our friends and most of all we learn from our own triumphs and idiocies. Millennial camp followers aside, though, we tend *not* to learn from strangers telling us how we ought to behave.

So I'm not going to try. Quite the contrary. What I want to discuss instead are the ways *your* code of ethics— be that code Christian, Jewish, or Moslem, environmentalist, humanist, or occupational (because, obviously, many jobs come equipped with their own extensive codes of behavior)— can be applied to the sloppy, ennobling business of business.

Provided you want to act well in the world, the following pages will help. Because if the derivation of ethical principles is a notoriously boggy subject, the life work of the seldom-read and centuries-dead, application of those principles to real-life challenges and decisions is rather more straightforward. Applying your own ethical beliefs is a matter of proceeding systematically. It's also a matter of practice. A word about "practice" in just a minute. The procedure, I think, should go something like this:

1. *I.D. your Id.* What do you stand to gain from this decision? What loss will you suffer? Asking yourself to be wholly immune to the siren song of self-interest is unrealistic. In some cases, it may even be unnecessary. But failing to

recognize and delimit your self-interest—failing, in other words, to look beyond your own desires at the rights and interests of other people—can lead to disastrous decision-making. As we shall see.

2. *Move to control time.* Write down the deadlines dictated by the situation. Do you have five minutes to make a plan? Can you wait a week? Are you acting as an independent agent, or is the timing of a transaction or market opportunity controlling *you*? If it's the latter, resist the influence. In financial matters, urgency is often the enemy of good conduct.

3. *Fight for the facts.* It doesn't matter how well-meaning you are. If you don't know the facts, you're not going to make a solid decision. Are you missing some important details of the event that is unfolding? Are you looking at the right questions? What additional information do you need? Don't be so proud of your assumptions. In the financial world, just as in medicine, law, and engineering, ignorance may itself be unethical.

4. *Consult.* Who can help you find a solution? Who's available? What special perspectives will you want to incorporate in addressing this particular issue? Think of gender/cultural differences, and the various areas of experience

and technical expertise a fully-informed decision will demand. Discount recommendations from people who don't know the details of the situation as well as you do.

5. *Identify the people your decision may affect.* Who will benefit from the choice you make? Who will be hurt? How and how much? Consider and *take responsibility for* the effects on others. Imagine the consequences of your action not just today, but a year from now. And ten years from now.

6. *List the workable alternatives and their consequences.* This is harder than you might imagine. Don't just list the obvious alternatives. Stretch yourself. Pilfer thoughts. Beg ideas. Press yourself to produce a genuinely broad range of options.

7. *Make a workable, understandable decision* that you believe embodies—and will be *perceived* as embodying—your ethical aspirations. Follow through. Modify the decision as the situation changes, and see that it's implemented by competent people who understand the ambitions behind the policy. Identify the lessons to be incorporated in corporate training, practice, and policy to make the next crisis a little less surprising.

The Bottom Rung

So that's the list. I can hear the hoots already. *Seven steps, huh? That's going to change my life?*

Of course not. Fact is, we ethicists are almost always preaching to the converted. The sort of people who read books about acting well are precisely the people most likely to figure out how to do it on their own. I'm not pretending *Values Added* will make you want to produce principled decisions, walk with the righteous and preserve civilization as we know it. I'm assuming you already do. Given this desire, I'm confident my procedural checklist will help. *Without* this desire, no quantity of coaching will move you. Might as well try teaching a tapeworm to tapdance. Stop reading.

Unfortunately, I have to admit at this point to one criticism of my earlier work I'm not sure I've corrected. In my writings I've focused on financial professionals who have hoisted themselves high enough in the corporate hierarchy to have the luxury of considering the ethical nuances of a given decision. In other words, the *big guys*. But what about the kids starting out in the bond-trading pits or manning the cold-call telephones, busting their butts 12 hours a day for some money-motivated sonofabitch who wouldn't know Immanuel Kant from George Jetson? A young trader on Wall Street recently described, for *New York* magazine, the environment in which he and his colleagues work: "The other day, this guy on the trading floor is sitting at his screen, watching the market move away from him. This is a lot of money he's going to lose. And he stands up and vomits all over the floor."

Aren't these first-years "financial professionals"? But it's sell or walk, and sometimes a sale can be helped along by an exaggeration, a half-truth, a flat-out whopper. And hey, everyone does it. So what relevance does an ethics casebook have for the new meat?

Values Added actually has more relevance for the rookie than for anyone else. Having worked in the financial industry for the last four decades, I realize that people make compromises all the time. Most of these compromises don't mean much by themselves. It's just that they start to add up. And worse, they get easier. Giving in to cynicism isn't worthwhile in the long run. Maybe you'll make some money. Maybe you'll own a nice apartment. But the lies will catch up to you eventually, or an angry customer will, and there will always be someone else available to sit at your desk, to stare at your screen, to mimic your migraines.

I'm not advocating a run at sainthood. I simply report what I've found—that a failure to hang onto some basic commitment to ethical behavior is a personal catastrophe, and as disabling to one's hopes of occupational advancement at a reputable firm as an inability to add and subtract. And that's true regardless of who's screaming at you today or how nice your name sounds on the hoot and holler.

Procedure

A word about chapters 3-14. Because straight narration can be tedious, I've chosen to present my points by means of imaginary folks in actual jobs, using a series of "documents": interviews, notes, diary entries, *etc.* of the people involved in the ethical dilemmas discussed. My hope is that the reader will study these documents the way a flatfoot follows evidence—piecing together story, motive, and character from the intentionally subjective clues I've provided. Most of these fables make "negative" points; that is, they illustrate what should have been done by showing what wasn't. Each case relates, more or less obviously, to one of the seven steps I've outlined above. My analysis following the fiction will make the connection clearer.

Preparation

Practice. I mentioned it earlier. Can you *practice* ethical behavior? Admittedly, nothing is going to prepare you fully for the glabrous beast outside, smacking lips that look like raw liver and claiming to be Life itself. But it *is* possible to study a number of ethical dilemmas—the temptations of inside information, the lure of "soft dollars"—that recur in financial matters. They're dilemmas that you'll have to wrestle with, just as I've had to and a hundred thousand other people before you. They're different from the ethical problems faced by a fireman, say, or a cowboy, or even a doctor. And they're not going to go away. But by understanding the elements of the problem, you can start to prepare for the problems themselves. By trying out solutions, by trying *yourself*, you take an even bigger step. And when the Beast raises its stinking head, at least you won't have to deal with shock. Just the stench.

Rules and Right

I've chosen not to examine the rules and regulations governing these problems for a couple of reasons. First, the law is constantly changing. Anything I write today about, say, the "safe harbor" exception for soft dollar transactions under Rule 28(e) of the Securities Exchange Act, stands a good chance of being obsolete tomorrow. Better to learn the intricacies of the problem, I think, than to memorize today's attempt to solve it.

Second, the law is beside the point. *Values Added* is about trying to make the *right* decision, which is often harder than simply making the legal decision.

And one final note. Though I've tried to avoid preaching, readers will no doubt notice my own principles and prejudices coloring the analyses of the cases that follow. I've reserved a brief discussion of my ideas about ethics for the final chapter of the book, to be read or not at the reader's discretion. It's the last chapter not as peroration but as a potential ad lib resource. After all, what matters most isn't my beliefs. It's yours.

Chapter 2

Three Perspectives:
Establishing Common Ground
for Ethical Judgments

Business ethics differs from purely personal ethics in that an individual employee has to consider not only his own interests but also those of his employer, and those of his employer's owners, the shareholders.

A s I indicated in my introduction, my interest is procedure. I'm not selling substance. You have to supply that yourself.

Still, in order to proceed with discussion of the cases to follow, it will help enormously to establish a common set of references. It seems to me that we can start by asking three questions to determine if the decision we're about to make is ethical: Does it *work*? Is it *fair*? And do those affected have a *voice*?

1. Does the Decision Work?

Financial professionals are practical people. Their work is generally measurable by numerical standards. The performance artist trying to decide exactly when during his act to set his shoes on fire and hurl himself into a vat of simulated blood is not going to be able to consult a bar graph to see if his decision—*late in the show, perhaps, just after that wrenching exploration of repressed Oedipal conflicts*—was the correct one.

That's not true for the bond trader. He has to make his numbers. He has clients to please. So it makes sense to begin our exploration of ethical judgments with the point of view of practicality, or *pragmatism*. In light of all the foreseeable effects and available alternatives, does a given decision work to the benefit of the decision-maker's employer?

For example, taking into account cost and financial reward, would it be practical for an oil company executive to leave a played-out field in a small African nation in an unrestored and possibly dangerous condition? In the short-term, the answer may very well be *yes*. Assume there are no regulations applicable to her conduct. In this case, why should our executive spend her shareholders' money to fix a series of perfectly good holes in the ground? Local children might make use of the declivities as nifty hidey-holes as they gambol away the warm afternoons. Or people could just throw junk in 'em.

But pragmatism is elastic. As the best business thinkers know, true pragmatism involves looking beyond short-term profit toward *long-term* viability. The concept encompasses not just the present but also the future: future risks, future costs, future opportunities. For example, does it make sense for our oil exec to leave outraged citizens behind if she thinks her company might some day want to pursue a second set of drilling operations in the country? Or drilling operations anywhere else, for that matter, if the conditions it leaves behind in Africa are truly bad? What sort of publicity—RARE RHINOS TRAPPED IN SLUDGE PIT— will the unrestored field generate in the international press? How will the company's more environmentally sensitive shareholders react to these stories? Self-interest is the soul of even the most enlightened pragmatism.

Maybe pragmatism is best described not as a goal but as a necessary *component* of any ethical business decision. Business ethics differs from purely personal ethics in that an individual employee has to factor in not only his own interests but also a) those of his employer, and b) those of his employer's *owners*, the shareholders—who are out there always, rolling naked on their dividend checks and disparaging the simplemindedness of corporate management everywhere. Basically, pragmatism dictates that any decision has to make sense, from as broad a financial perspective as possible, for the company. Even Ben & Jerry's, that burr in the blanket of corporate conservatism, recognizes that one of its primary duties is, along with saving the world, "increasing value for our shareholders."

Securities analysts increasingly emphasize the importance of long-term thinking and stable customer relationships in the success of any corporate enterprise. Call it "enlightened pragmatism." Call it common sense. Most people would agree that it's smarter to make a profit of $100 five times with a customer than it is to fleece that customer out of $250 once. From this perspective, it's obvious that an unethical decision may be unpragmatic. It can destroy business relationships. It can hurt a company's long-term viability.

What's more important is realizing that, at least as far as an employee's duties to his managers, shareholders, and customers are concerned, an impractical decision may itself be unethical. No stockbroker can play Sir Thomas More, ready to sacrifice all in pursuit of principle. It's not all his to sacrifice. Absolute stands, extravagant screeds, retreats to Saskatchewan hamlets—they're fine things, all, and testament to muscular hearts. But they're irrelevant here. Take it as credo, cliche, capstone, commandment: an ethical *business* decision has to make sense for the business.

2. Is the Decision Fair to Those Concerned?

Back to our oil company scenario. Say the played-out African field in question is in a remote region. Its inhabitants have been known to kill strangers who try to photograph them and are so benighted as to be wholly distrustful of journalists, whom they refer to, in their delightful local dialect, as "pinheads." Assume, in short, that there's no chance of our energy outfit ever being linked with the problems of this small field. Pragmatically, it makes perfect sense for the corporation to cut and run. *What's to stop it?*

A commitment to justice might.

Without belaboring the concept, justice can be said to require "fair dealing" or "due rewards." Individual answers to questions of fairness may of course differ. But the questions themselves are obvious. Is it *fair* for our oil company to leave inhabitants of the area with a contaminated water table, ruined fields, and leaky pipelines?

Maybe it is. Maybe local representatives very shrewdly bargained for exorbitant land-lease fees from the company in an explicit attempt to accumulate a fund for clean-up of the site after the company finished piercing it. Unlikely? Yes. But what does it do to our question? Given these facts, maybe the company isn't being so "unjust" after all in declining to mop up its mess.

Different companies have widely different commitments to the nebulous idea of justice. Some—Levi-Strauss and Ben & Jerry's, to name only two—have wide-ranging corporate beliefs in this regard. Other perfectly reputable enterprises are governed with Milton Friedman's influential exhortation in mind: "There is one and only one social responsibility of business—to use its resources and engage in activities designed to increase its profits so long as it stays within the rules of the game, which is to say, engages in open and free competition without deception or fraud." The point to keep in mind here is that considerations of justice, as opposed to mere pragmatism, will be more or less applicable depending on the ethos of the company you work for—though as you rise higher in the corporate hierarchy, you will have increasing opportunities not merely to comply with this corporate ethos but to re-create it.

In an era when social justice concerns are often voiced, if not always acted on, cynics may argue that it is increasingly pragmatic for a company to act, or at least appear to act, justly. You don't have to give a damn. You just have to *say* you give a damn. It helps sell products: soft drinks, senators, sweaters, soup. Though there's a grain of truth to this observation, it seems to me that considerations of pragmatism and justice continue to be conflicting perspectives, at least at the margins, and that both ought to be factored into the ethical decision.

3. *Do Those Affected Have a Voice?*

From the corporate perspective, justice is something good done to, or for, others. The idea of respecting rights, on the other hand, involves letting others do for *themselves*: speak for themselves, act for themselves, bring forward their own solutions.

Returning once again to our rutted oil field, we can ask what would happen if the energy company in question were to decide that, despite the limited nature of its contractual obligations and the minimal risk of any negative media fall-out, it would like to restore completely its played-out wells and at least stretch a few tarps over those toxic sludge pits. What's more, the company has decided that it will fund its innovative Western educational program for the children of native employees for another 20 years.

Certainly all of this seems fair to an outsider. But what if it turns out that the provincial government doesn't give a damn—despite the concerns of local residents—about what it sees as the small-scale pollution problems generated by the company's drilling operations? What if the government is more concerned about the fact that the roads the company paved to allow access to the oil field are cracking in the sub-Saharan heat? What if aardvarks are eating the asphalt? What if what the government *really* wants is enough road maintenance equipment and training to allow it to keep up and expand the region's infrastructure? And what if local residents are not only unimpressed but actually annoyed by the Western-style teaching—*hopelessly monotheistic, they think, and thus antithetical to ancient traditions*—going on at the oil company's school?

In this situation, whose preferences should be taken into account? And if preferences differ, whose should be given more weight?

The point for us isn't to answer these questions. We can leave that to the officers and directors of our now-embattled oil company, and gently shut the boardroom door. The point is that what *we* consider to be perfectly just and fair may seem irrelevant or even burdensome to those afflicted by our fine intentions—those who, because they are human beings, with the usual complement of ambitions, resentments, and runny noses, are not as easily dealt with as statistical projections.

Admittedly, concern with the rights of others may be seen as a subset of a broader concern with acting justly in the world, just as at least a minimal concern with "justice" may be seen as a necessary component of enlightened pragmatism in these days of environmental and racial crankiness. Still, I think that examining a given situation from the three perspectives of acting pragmatically, doing justice, and respecting rights can lead to three slightly different pictures of that situation—and of the best way to address it.

Which, incidentally, is just what we want. Not the jumble but the competition. Of interests. Of rights. Of responsibilities. And what I as a writer would most like to do now is give you an ethical calculus, a formula that would enable you always to do the right thing by all concerned. But don't hold your breath. The right decision in the cases to come doesn't stand like the x in a schoolboy's equation. It's more like the result of oceanic navigation. We know where we want to go, and we have certain fixed points, as well as numerous variable influences, to help or hinder us as we travel. We get better with practice.

And maybe, just maybe, that's land looming ahead.

Two Cases

I have some experience with this sort of navigation. By way of relating it, let me first ask you to consider the following scenario.

The management of a company we'll call Middleton Genetics feels threatened by an outsider's proposal to buy the company for cash. Management therefore proposes to its Board of Directors a set of five-year employment contracts between the company and each of its seven top executives. These contracts call for nearly tripling each individual's current benefits if and when there is an unfriendly merger and the executives are given the boot.

The President of Middleton argues that (a) such an account payable will slow down any unfriendly takeover; (b) the Board will be able to act at its own pace and in the best interests of Middleton in any negotiations with the prospective buyer; (c) no financial burden is being placed on Middleton, as the contingent costs will be borne by the acquiring company, not the current shareholders; and (d) the executives will, by virtue of being deemed worthy of these new contracts, be receiving a vote of confidence that will help them do a good job in managing the company.

This type of employment contract, the familiar "golden parachute," can be an effective tool in discouraging tender offers—and in launching the managers in question on a golden yacht should a merger occur. But are the President's statements convincing? Is anyone a loser here? You don't have to be a genius to see that the private interest of the executives concerned is clearly at the heart of the proposal. Because of the personal ties that frequently bind managers and directors, the Board may in turn feel predisposed to bless the arrangement.

This is not to imply that any merger proposal should be accepted *posthaste*, and current management sent packing; merely that it is always a good idea to apply a discount factor to points made with a sizeable component of self-interest. Specifically, the Board needs to test whether it is in the interest of Middleton as a whole (not just management, but also the company's employees and shareholders) to slow down or frighten away this or any takeover effort. What's the likely price per share? What's the price of the employment agreements? Nothing is free. If the acquiring company has to pay off the executives, some of that money will almost certainly be diverted from the target shareholders. These, of course, are precisely the people Middleton's execs should be trying hardest to serve.

The Real Thing

The bottom line is that term employment contracts can help a corporation attract and retain top people or they can result in pork-barrel deals. The key difference lies in the facts upon which the management decision concerning the agreements is based.

I learned this distinction firsthand in 1980, when the issue was presented to those of us then serving on the Board of Directors of Cavitron Corporation. Cavitron had sales of around $40 million and stock listed on the American Exchange. The company owned a number of excellent specialized products, including a state-of-the-art method for outpatient removal of cataracts and a laser surgery device with potential for breakthrough cancer surgery. Several years of high interest rates and inflation, slow payment by customers, and difficulties with inventory control had depressed the company's stock price to under $10 a share, despite a coincident expansion of sales. But these problems were temporary. Cavitron eventually emerged from these difficulties with very attractive earning estimates, and its stock started moving.

Then came a suitor, Cooper Laboratories, an aggres-sively-managed public company with some complementary products, a controversial CEO, and a history of forced ac-quisitions. Though we on the Cavitron board didn't want to sell out or merge, we knew we had a responsibility to listen to the suitor's proposal. We also concluded it was likely that Cavitron's management team would be deemed redun-dant if Cooper's overture was successful. This meant that the executives' justifiable concern for their careers and com-pensation could seriously influence their ability to manage regular business, let alone negotiate the best deal for their shareholders.

Up to that point, Cavitron's key executives had never worked under written employment contracts. In the face of Cooper's interest, though, the company's independent directors, led by Chairman William G. Weld, initiated a proposal for term contracts for several of Cavitron's senior officers. The agreements Bill Weld initiated were not contingent but immediate. Compensation was set at the salaries currently being paid. The term was three years.

And they worked.

Cavitron's management remained with the company during a stressful period of hot and cold negotiations, ultimately brokering a cash deal with Cooper Laboratories at a level three times the trading price at the beginning of the exercise. Obviously, the deal turned out well for the shareholders. On the other hand, the key Cavitron executives did lose their jobs. Their employment contracts ("bronze parachutes"?) weren't overly generous, but they did provide a timely psychological bonus for the executives during the negotiations, a bridge period after the deal was struck, and a result that was helpful to both shareholders and executives.

The Point of All This

The starting point for the Cavitron board was not how to block a known deal, but rather how to help those who were on the spot to act in the shareholders' interest, accepting or rejecting the tender offer as the facts required. Reducing the actions of the board to the ethical categories we'll be using in the rest of *Values Added*, the directors looked at the practical interests of the corporation, not fetishistically (in terms of the people currently running the place, or the company's names or trademarks) but as a vehicle for investment and production, trying to balance the desires of its shareholders and employees in a concerned way.

The Board's actions were also *just*: Cavitron's officers received compensation that helped them to act with dignity and deliberation even as they went about ending their own jobs.

Finally, I feel the actions we took were respectful of the *rights* of those involved. Rather than being shut out by a prohibitively expensive set of golden parachute provisions, the officers and shareholders of Cooper Laboratories were allowed to make their case for merger, while the officers and shareholders of Cavitron were allowed (in the case of the officers, *encouraged*) to listen.

No regulatory scheme spelled out the steps for the Cavitron Board to take in the event of merger negotiations. A group of concerned people simply analyzed the situation, thought hard, and came up with a workable conclusion. It's possible. I've seen it.

A positive result like this reverberates. Whether the reason stems from the self-interest of enlightened pragmatism or from a true commitment to fairness, financial professionals who exercise due regard for the interests of others increase the likelihood that regulators will treat them as persons of integrity, now and in the future. The converse is also true: managers who act as though deregulation has erased public policy have missed the point and will press government to reenter the arena of private business. Moreover, the concerned professional who is on the spot and knows the facts can often do better than government in terms of applying ethics and balancing conflicting interests to achieve a general social benefit. Where there's a will, there's a way.

Now for the way.

I.D. Your Id

It was a filthy profession, but the money was addicting, and one addiction led to another, and they were all going to hell.

Po Bronson
Bombardiers

Chapter 3

Ambition as Amphetamine:
Self-Interest vs.
The Interests of Others (1996)

The use of military and sporting metaphors in American business is at an all-time high. Deals are battles. Competitors—sometimes even customers— are enemies.

Values Added isn't concerned with the case of the mild-mannered accountant who empties his client's trust account and hops the first jet for Paraguay. That's simple theft, and any reader who needs to puzzle out why our *accountant's* actions are unethical has some catching up to do. But self-interest comes also in subtler shapes, as the following events suggest.

Meet Rusty Merrick, until very recently one of MidWest Mutual Bank's brightest stars. Merrick's record sparkles like a Hill Country creek. He put together a 3.82 GPA in obtaining his B.S. in Business from the University of Texas, worked two years as a management consultant in Dallas, then bagged an MBA from Rice. After graduation, he moved north to join the loan department at MidWest, where he promptly won a name for himself.

Rusty's first initiative involved assisting Deer Field Tools, one of MidWest's largest loan customers, to ward off a hostile takeover bid by Boston-based Massachusetts Conglomerates. The head of MidWest's loan department gave Merrick the green light for helping Deer Field. He even provided back-up coverage to handle Merrick's other responsibilities within the department, allowing the young executive to devote all his energy to the takeover defense.

Merrick on camera:

> I look at that whole thing as a sort of trial by fire. First blood, right? Second week of May, MassCon made an S.E.C. filing to the effect that they'd acquired 5 percent of Deer Field's stock. And they had to explain their plans, but they didn't tell us much. Said the acquisition was for "investment purposes only." We all knew better than that. They wanted control.

> First thing I did was read everything I could find about both companies. It was clear that MassCon saw Deer Field's local operations as a convenient source of cash. After they took over, I figured they'd close down the local plants, sell off the inventory and patents, and come out ahead. We at MidWest would lose one of our best customers and get squat out of MassCon. The question was, *how could we keep Deer Field independent?*

I had role-played the bad guy in a couple of M&A simulations in graduate school, and read a lot in the papers about tender offers and takeovers. So I really jumped into the middle of it. Deer Field realized I knew what I was doing. They'd have jumped off a cliff if I told 'em to. Instead I recommended to the treasurer of Deer Field that management be issued a new class of convertible preferred stock with 50 votes per share on any acquisition proposal, with the obvious result that management would have a stronger voice. It was an old shark repellent. The company had had the power on the books for years. Only problem was, no one ever had the money to take advantage of it. Now MidWest was going to supply that money.

Our in-house lawyers gave me the nod on Plan A and also cleared my idea that Deer Field contribute some of that convertible preferred to MidWest as trustee of the company's pension fund, instead of making their annual cash contribution. This was to add more votes and free up some bucks for use against MassCon.

So everything is looking copacetic, we're gonna kick ourselves some Yankee butt, when all of a sudden a little bombshell comes whistling in. It's a memo from this feeb Elaine Tolland, who manages Deer Field's pension fund for the bank, putting up some static about taking the preferred. I get a copy. The President of MidWest gets a copy. About the only person Elaine *doesn't* cc is Alan Greenspan. Of course I saved the damn thing:

...I agree that the bank's interest in protecting Deer Field against MassCon's takeover bid is important to us all. I also recognize that there are many ways in which the interests of the employees and management of Deer Field come together. However, there are different interests in the pension fund, and the U.S. Labor Department requires that all such funds be managed in the sole interest of the retirement-income security beneficiaries.

My chief fiduciary concern is with our proposed acceptance of the company's unmarketable preferred stock. Pension fund investments must be reviewed and documented. There are significant valuation questions here, especially in light of the current financial pressures on Deer Field. If the preferred is transferred to the Deer Field trust, it may be necessary for the trust department to exclude it from our fee so we don't have to guarantee its current market value. In any event, we may have a responsibility to watch over the preferred and need to evaluate all the relevant risks and opportunities.

Nice, huh? One of my own people trying to frag me. For a couple of hours the senior guys were all concerned and I had to rally the troops. They called a big meeting, very serious, and after a brief opportunity for everyone to smile at each other, they threw me and Elaine into the ring. It was pretty intense. She—*well, hell.* Take a look at the transcript.

Tolland: At the risk of repetition, I have to say that I feel like our first job here should be to spell out the interest of the Deer Field pension fund. The specific issue that faces us as their trustee is can we accept—much less *welcome*—unmarketable securities to fund the retirement income of Deer Field employees? The risks and opportunities land on the pension's *beneficiaries*, not on Deer Field's management.

Merrick: Maybe that's true. But you're missing the big picture. What's the risk to your beneficiaries if MassCon takes over and just decides to shut down the company and terminate the pension fund altogether?

Tolland: What if it does? Maybe we should explore the point.

Merrick: Fine. Somebody call Lewis and Clark. In the meantime, we're about to lose one of our best clients.

Tolland: I don't appreciate your tone of voice, Rusty. Tell me this. You know Deer Field's financials. Can the company pay the pension benefits?

Merrick: You know as well as I do, there's a surplus in the pension fund.

Tolland: Okay. Fine. Then the risks of the plan taking the preferred stock is considerably less. But what if Deer Field at some future point *doesn't* have an independent capacity to pay the retirements? What if MassCon eventually wins, and liquidates its new conquest? The beneficiaries look to us as trustee of the plan's assets and those assets had better be good.

Merrick: You want objectivity. Fine. On a strictly objective basis, what's the risk of our taking the Deer Field preferred? Deer Field is a big company. We lend it a lot of money. The bank buys its commercial paper in our cash management group.

Tolland: But not for our *trust* customers. Not now. The quality's not high enough.

Merrick: The quality's not high enough? Are you kidding me? One of our biggest clients, and we won't even buy its stock to keep it from disappearing?

Tolland: Not if it's junk.

Merrick: Look, Elaine. This isn't just common stock. It's preferred and convertible—the best of both worlds. What if Deer Field doesn't contribute *anything* to the fund this year? You keep forgetting about the loss of jobs out there if MassCon takes over.

Tolland: We're paid to be fiduciaries, and to protect this pension fund. Of course I'm concerned about jobs and our business relationship with the sponsor. But a lot of people at that company are relying on us to protect their retirement money. That's all they *have*, for God's sake, and we have to safeguard that side of their lives before we help Deer Field beat off this takeover attempt. There's probably a lot of overlap between those who now work at the company and those who will be beneficiaries of the pension plan. But don't forget their wives and children. And even if we find a way of taking the preferred stock, you talk about actually going out and buying Deer Field common in the marketplace.

Merrick: Well, take a look. The price is going up every day.

Tolland: The price is up because of the take-over bid! The question is, will it stay up over the long term? We have to ask if this is a fair price to pay and if we'll be able to sell at a profit after this unusual environment is over. And don't count on all those extra votes either, Rusty. I'll bet MassCon will be in court looking for an order that the pension fund not be allowed to vote any of these shares.

***

You get the idea. I have to admit, Elaine Tolland is no pushover. I also have to admit I walked right into that one about buying the common on the open market. But I'm no pushover, either, and basically what I did finally is point out that MidWest has a very solid legal department. They all drive Volvos and they're so up-to-date on all the government regs that they won't sharpen a pencil without filing forms with the FDIC. And they cleared all my proposals. So what were we worried about?

That was when our CEO nodded. You know, one of those magisterial nods, like he's just decided to let you live. And I knew I had him.

So we went ahead. MidWest even lent money at prime to a few of the key people over there to make it easy for them to buy Deer Field common on the open market and the new preferred directly from the company. What a combination that was. It really slowed MassCon down and we were able to take some additional steps then because we had more time: stock options to the executives, a new 401(k) option to buy Deerfield common (and control the vote). We got the union fund for the hourly workers in on the act, too. It was a kick. As you may know from reading the papers at the time, we won. MassCon had gobbled up 19 percent of the stock by the end of the battle, but that was about it. They didn't have the votes they needed, so they sold their shares, took their losses, and moved on to other targets.

I'd shown—I mean, *we'd* shown—how an imaginative, aggressive bank can help its clients, and word like that really gets around. In fact, I think the MassCon battle had a lot to do with my getting the job here at Chemical and, you know, joining the big-time. Uh, excuse me. Can you sit tight for a second? I've got to take this call.

Reaction:

_____

_____

_____

_____

_____

_____

_____

_____

_____

_____

_____

_____

_____

_____

Body Count

Self-interest is sometimes difficult to distinguish from legitimate professional zeal. Rusty Merrick's is a classic case. Here's an intelligent young man doing his considerable best to "save" one of his bank's best loan customers. Merrick doesn't profit personally from these loans. Losing Deer Field to Massachusetts Conglomerates isn't going to mean any immediate reduction in his salary or benefits. And yet it's easy to see the selfishness in his campaign to thwart MassCon's takeover attempt.

Still, even given that Merrick's actions are at least in part ego-driven, is there anything *unethical* about what he's done? Let's start with our three points of view. First, practicality. All things considered, has Merrick acted in accordance with the best interests of his employer? The short-term benefits of preserving Deer Field as an independent bank customer are fairly obvious. For one thing, the bank gets more loan business. And Merrick alludes at one point to another, longer-term benefit. He feels it will be advantageous for MidWest to gain a reputation as the sort of bank that is willing to come to the defense of a customer threatened with a change of ownership.

Yet there's at least one MidWest employee who sees strong disadvantages to the bank and its customers in Merrick's campaign. As Elaine Tolland points out, the bank is also paid to safeguard the interests of the pension beneficiaries for whom the bank acts as fiduciary. Her point is that accepting securities of questionable value in order to keep Deer Park independent may be overreaching. Let's assume Deer Field's loan business is considerably more valuable to MidWest than its (Deer Field's) pension management account. Does this justify the bank's favoring the loan account in a way that undercuts its duty as pension manager? And if so, is the justification a matter of relative revenues and relative costs?

What if Tolland were to raise this objection: If Deer Field can place unmarketable issues of stock with its pension fund in this instance, it may encourage other pension fund sponsors to try the same thing with even less desirable securities. The fact that one action is just within the bounds of propriety this time may make it difficult for the bank to make a principled objection to a proposed transfer that is just over the line of *impropriety* next time. Does this tip the scale of the bank's long-term interests—our concerns of practicality, or pragmatism—against Merrick's determined guerilla tactics?

Machine Gun Nation

Here's a related but perhaps less urgent question. Is Merrick's behavior good for the bank in an internal sense? Look at his use of military metaphor. In his own mind he's a dashing cavalry officer, J.E.B. Stuart incarnate, George Patton rumbling over the Rhine. He sees questions from another executive—a more senior executive, in fact—as "fragging" by one of his "soldiers." Is this the way a bank ought to be run? Is this the way any financial organization should be run?

Unfortunately, the use of military tropes in business is at an all-time high. In Joseph Heller's classic *Catch-22*, we laugh at the entrepreneurial Major Milo Minderbinder because he insists on seeing the Second World War as an opportunity for the exchange of mutually beneficial products and services. War, in other words, is business. In his greatest coup, Minderbinder strikes a deal to bomb his own airfield on behalf of the Germans because he can do it cheaper than they can.

And strafe it as well? asks one of his men.

"'We have no choice,' Milo informed him resignedly. 'It's in the contract.'"

The idea of war as business is often reversed in contemporary America. Deals are battles. Competitors, and sometimes even customers, are enemies. In his 1995 novel *Bombardiers*, a former securities salesman named Po Bronson parodies this tendency mercilessly. His harried bond traders

> humped out to their foxholes, hunkered down, got combat-ready, dropped their bombs, waited for the faceless enemy. At the end of the day, when tallying up their trading tickets, they were 'counting scalps.' The 1987 stock market crash was the Bomb, and time was measured Before the Bomb/After the Bomb, as if the market had never rebounded from that ominous day. The money market desk was staffed by grunts, while Green Berets roved the mortgage desk.

It all makes for a coercive, joyless, ultimately unproductive place of business. And what if, instead of voicing her concerns humanely, Elaine Tolland were to adopt the military mindset of her colleague Merrick? What if she were determined to fight for the prerogatives of her pension management department as frenetically as Merrick argues for *his* goals? What sort of battlefield would the bank be then?

There's no question that the barracks ethos can help people achieve short-term goals—taking out that enemy SCUD site, for example, or selling another penny stock to some defenseless retiree in Daytona. What militaristic thinking tends to inhibit is serious consideration of why those short-term goals are important. Don't fall into the trap. Listen to people—even people you're tempted to think of as your enemies. Make up your own mind. No nation is waiting to thank you for your territorial conquests, your corporate kills. As obvious as it may seem, the points bear repeating:

You are not a conscript.

Finance ain't a war.

Considering the Equities

Fairness involves looking outward. Rusty Merrick's primary focus in the MassCon takeover bid was on the management of Deer Field and the financial interests of MidWest. But there are other interests worth considering here. For example, has Merrick looked adequately at the interests of MidWest's shareholders? Their capital is at risk in several ways. Apart from the potential loss of a major customer, there are significant liability risks in connection both with bringing the unmarketable preferred stock into one of MidWest's pension funds and in lending money to Deer Field's key executives, especially if this lending is based on the pension fund relationship. Merrick's specific comments about the bank's legal department suggest he thinks that his professional responsibilities need not rise above a legal minimum. Do you agree?

Does the bank have responsibilities to anyone else other than its shareholders? Even apart from considering Deer Field as a corporate loan customer, what about Deer Field's many employees in the area? Some of them may be MidWest customers as well. Sizeable lay-offs are likely to hurt the local economy as a whole. So what sort of concerns can MidWest legitimately express in connection with the takeover issue? And should they be balanced by a concern for the *shareholders* of Deer Park, who may also be customers of MidWest, and who stand to gain significantly if MassCon makes a high enough bid for their shares? Is MidWest acting fairly toward *them*? Does it have any obligation to do so?

And finally, does MidWest have any responsibility to the American economy? A responsibility, say, to safeguard investor interest in free alienability of property and open competition among companies? What if MassCon is simply a better-run business than Deer Field? What if, in some sense, Deer Field *deserves* to be taken over? Without more facts, answering such questions is impossible. But it would increase the ethical credibility of MidWest's actions immeasurably if we could see that *someone* at the bank had asked, and tried to answer, them.

Listening to Those Concerned

Great. So now we've identified a host of groups that may be affected by Rusty Merrick's campaign in support of Deer Field Tool. It isn't practical to poll each constituent of these groups on MidWest's strategy. And even if it *were* practical, how much weight should be accorded to each group? What if members of the same group disagreed about the strategy?

Trying to respect the rights of all those affected by a financial decision is often easier said than done. Still, it's not impossible. Merrick or his superiors at the bank—who seem, in this case, to have been about as active as hothouse tomatoes—might contact representative members of the affected groups. Elaine Tolland is actually a perfect representative for one group, Deer Field's pension beneficiaries. Rusty Merrick's disregard for her suggestions is typical of a general disdain for the rights of others often seen in actions with a high degree of self-interest.

Merrick himself, now perched comfortably in a fine office of Chemical Bank, surveying the fabled maze of Manhattan from 50 floors up, might not feel he has anything to regret in his handling of the MassCon takeover attempt. All things considered, perhaps his campaign made sense. A telephone call to the Missouri city where Rusty Merrick briefly lived and worked reveals that Deer Field is still in business. In fact the company is doing nicely, employing people, faithfully funding its pension plan, and returning to MidWest Mutual for its short-term borrowing needs.

And maybe the final questions to be asked here are these: Was Merrick really worried about Deer Field's interests, or was he promoting his own? Do you feel as satisfied with his actions as he does? And—*most importantly*—would you have done the same?

Chapter 4

The Boesky Syndrome: Appropriating Information for Personal Use (1992)

Insider trading—the embezzlement of information— is the financial world's most pervasive sin.

Insider trading is the embezzlement of information. Only one step removed from material theft, it is the financial world's most pervasive sin. But despite periodic high-profile indictments and the subsequent bouts of journalistic bedwetting such indictments tend to inspire, there is little public understanding of why insider trading is ethically wrong.

This confusion is unsurprising. Academics disagree on the issue, and even *The Wall Street Journal* has opined more than once that because insider trading makes for a more efficient market and better pricing system, it ought to be legal. Many Americans apparently agree. Despite the sorry example of Ivan Boesky and a host of his less prominent pupils, the practice of insider trading is, as *Business Week* recently put it, "alive and well—and growing."

For Those Who Missed the 80s

A couple of quick hypotheticals will serve to illustrate the ethical questions involved. Imagine the board of directors of XCO (corporate motto, "Bet You Never Thought You'd Own One of *These!*") decides to raise the company's annual dividend based on a surprisingly good earnings report. A rash of handshakes breaks out. Someone orders more danish. And a director named Marty Browne excuses himself during a coffee break to telephone his ophthalmologist. Secretly, though, Browne phones his broker instead, instructing the broker to buy a truckload of XCO common for his (Browne's) personal account.

So begins your garden-variety insider trading case. Note the obvious sneakiness, the strong whiff of self-interest, the equally pungent odor of stupidity. Unlike most insiders, Browne stands an excellent chance of being caught.

Legalities aside, though, is there anything wrong with his actions? Using knowledge he's acquired because his duties as director include representing XCO's shareholders, Browne is personally profiting in a transaction with one of his constituents, a selling shareholder who lacks similar knowledge. On the other hand, he didn't *induce* that shareholder to sell. The shareholder would have sold her shares anyway, receiving the same amount from another buyer that she has now received from Browne. No one can complain. No one was hurt. *Right?* So why is this trade ethically wrong?

The easy answer is to say that Marty Browne is a "fiduciary." The word is important in financial matters, where it refers to someone who undertakes to act for the benefit of another person or persons in any of a range of activities. Trustees are fiduciaries. So are the executors of estates. Corporate officers and directors are fiduciaries with respect to their shareholders, and we expect them to put the interests of those shareholders first.

But saying that Browne acted improperly because he was a fiduciary begs an important question. Why is it that we expect him to act as a fiduciary to begin with? How are a shareholder's interests at risk here?

A Victimless Crime?

As the scholar Jennifer Moore has pointed out, broad prohibitions against insider trading make sense primarily in the context of long-term market efficiency. Without such prohibitions, an officer or director would have a strong incentive to keep important news from his shareholders—at least until he could arrange to trade on the news himself. This is the ethical conflict at the heart of insider trading: a constant temptation to delay disclosure of facts to the people whose interests you're supposed to be tending.

There are practical problems as well. As Moore sees it, a system that encouraged executives to focus less on running the business and more on manipulating information about that business could produce serious financial side-effects. For example, corporate managers might spend more time arranging profitmaking opportunities for themselves than on steadily growing the business. Investors might shy away from investing in a shady market, which would in turn erode the ability of American industry to finance its future.

Would our analysis differ if Marty Browne were to tip his *mother* to buy the XCO stock? What if he told a buddy? Assume he doesn't plan to make a personal profit from either purchase. Browne is presumably still getting some benefit out of doing a service for a relative or friend, even if this benefit is solely psychic. Is this enough to create a conflict of interest? Does it matter if Browne benefits *at all*?

One more step. Suppose Browne tells a securities analyst at Merrill Lynch about XCO's contemplated dividend hike before that hike has been publicly announced. What about the analyst? Is it fair to restrict the actions of people who are paid to sift the soil of daily information in search of financial ore? An analyst (whose job it is to ferret out facts from company officials and their customers) is part of the important process of disseminating material financial information, thus helping to make America's markets more efficient. She owes no allegiance to XCO's shareholders. So why can't she do what she wants?

Indictable Idealism

The following monologue comes courtesy of an anonymously-submitted dictaphone tape, believed to be the property of 29-year-old Mary Colavito, formerly a securities analyst for a Florida-based investment management company called Coyne Portfolio Services.

Time to think fast here, Mary. After all, your job is on the line. In half an hour you're going to have to walk into Frederick W. DeClerk's office and justify yourself to that pompous ass. Tell him exactly what you've done for the Special Schools pension plan and why it isn't cause to bounce a gal out of the company and into the trash like yesterday's news.

I'll take it from the top. We analysts are supposed to think of ourselves as officers of the securities markets, responsible for their well-being. And just in case that's not clear enough, Coyne has supplied us all with a set of rules on the subject. I suppose I should at least take a look at it before the meeting.

Policy on Inside Information

1. The firm will not use material inside information concerning the value or price of stocks when making decisions in accounts.

2. If you believe you may have received such information, try to determine if there really is a problem. Did the information come from the company on a confidential basis so that you are bound by the same restrictions and loyalties that bind your source? Is it still confidential? Is it important information or is it just a minor detail?

3. If you determine that you have in fact received material inside information, don't use it, and don't spread the news. Don't tell your clients or colleagues. Keep them free and able to use *public* information while you discuss a constructive course of action with someone in our legal department.

4. If there is a problem, try to work out a way to let our clients come out as well as if we *hadn't* received the prohibited information.

5. Remember, stock manipulators sometimes spread disinformation in order to create confusion while they buy or sell under their own plan. There may be a reason why you're hearing supposedly "confidential" information. It's better for our clients if you stop the person from telling you the tip before you hear it.

So much for the rules. I can't say I'm crazy about 'em, but I generally just keep my mouth shut and march right along like a good little storm trooper. For example, one time I received some inside dope on a plant closing by a company whose shares I'd recommended for one of our biggest clients. Obviously, it was in my client's interest to sell. But under the rules, I couldn't just dump the stock without explanation and be done with it. I thought of feeding the shares out in small lots and explaining the move as a cut in stocks—which it would have been. But how am I going to explain a nifty move like that if those friendly folks from the SEC come a' knockin'? What was my motivation? Lee Strasberg, are you out there?

Finally I went to DeClerk, who decided our best course of action was to tip off a reporter at the *Herald* about the story. It wasn't exactly Pulitzer Prize material, but she did write it up and when the details appeared in the paper the next day, we had a legitimate excuse to get rid of the stock. We didn't tell our client we'd had to go through this Mickey Mouse routine, and it seems like there ought to be a better way to do business. We could have spread the rumor ourselves, I suppose, but then everyone except our fee-paying client would have benefited. Or maybe we could have tried to get the *company* to release the information. But how were we going to put pressure on the company to do that when we weren't even supposed to have the information ourselves?

When you see news stories about insider trading, you get the sense that everybody is supposed to have the same amount of information. Not only is that impossible. It would put us all out of business. Bribing someone at a company to pass you the inside scoop is one thing, but what if a friendly VP calls you and says, "We just filed a report and on page 93 I think you'll find something interesting"? What do you do about that if it's *big*? It isn't fair to your customers to be so much of a prude that you ignore your responsibilities to them. Is it?

And bad news can be just as important as good. Let's say I learn that the whole crowd at a given company is crooked and I go to the S.E.C. like that guy Ray Dirks did back in 1967 about Equity Funding. I tell the regulators what I've learned and they just sit on their hands. What can I do? I can't call a press conference. I could get sued for slander and so could the firm. But on the other hand, I don't see how I can treat my customers fairly if I just stand pat and let them swing in the wind. My customers look to me to take care of them, to use my best investment judgment. It's *their* interests I'm looking after, not mine. I don't make an extra dime.

And what if I know of an account that could really use a break? The Special Schools pooled pension fund, for example. You think a bunch of schoolteachers and physical therapists are going to get good market information on a timely basis? Right. These people work their hearts out for some very unfortunate children. Children with Autism. M.S. AIDS. Children with "challenges," as they say now.

So what if an analyst uses confidential information to help out the little guy every once in awhile? What if a close friend in the business told me that a certain aerospace contractor was about to have a major space station contract pulled out from under it for poor performance? And that contractor B—*there's only a couple of them left, after all*—was going to inherit the work? And what if I passed on that information to our manager of small pension funds? How is that insider trading?

I'm not Edward Krasnoff. I read in the *Journal* where he and his cronies used to stand around on Krasnoff's yacht and swap stories about the companies they were outside directors for. There weren't any bags of cash. No secret drop spots. Just a bunch of Park Avenue types sipping secrets with their Schnapps, trading information about billion dollar companies the same way someone like me talks about how to get a ketchup stain out of her best blue blouse. And the thing of it is, no one caught Ed Krasnoff. The SEC didn't, like, *detect* him with their fancy computers. An angry ex-lover finally turned in one of Krasnoff's friends. In other words, someone snitched. Otherwise he'd still be doing dirty trades today.

I don't have a goddamn yacht, and neither do the people I'm trying to help. I'm just trying to make sure that for one brief shining moment, the market distributes its wealth a little more evenly. What's wrong with *that*?

Frankly, I don't understand the fuss. But I'm pretty sure Freddie DeClerk is about to explain it to me.

Reaction:

_____

_____

_____

_____

_____

_____

_____

_____

_____

_____

_____

_____

_____

_____

More About Colavito@Coyne.org

Corporate lawyer-turned-novelist Harvey Sawikin wrote a piece for the *New York Times* not long ago about a young attorney at one of Wall Street's finest firms. Though the kid was outwardly upright, a model associate, it turned out that he had in fact executed a long series of illegal trades based on information he received while engaged in the firm's mergers & acquisitions work. He'd shared the profits—hundreds of thousands of dollars' worth—with his unemployed brother. Shared them, that is, until the SEC caught up with him.

Sawikin wondered what motivates a guy with a robust career and annual earnings around 200 grand to become a thief. He then answered his own question. It may have had to do, he speculated, with the desire he himself once felt when he was doing similar work. He wanted to be a hero, to give gifts to people—a struggling relative, a long-time friend—who needed them more than he did. After all, the gift was only information. It was difficult to see any victims. What was wrong with that? And if *The Wall Street Journal* tells us maybe inside trading isn't so bad after all, why shouldn't we do it?

Which brings us to Mary Colavito. Why can't *she* help the little guy every once in awhile? In what sense is she acting out of "self-interest" here?

Ignore what the law says for a moment. When it comes to insider trading, the courts are hopelessly confused. Maybe the place to start is with the three perspectives on ethical behavior we talked about in Chapter 2. What about the practical results? Are Colavito's actions going to benefit Coyne Portfolio Services? In the short run, maybe they will. At least one client will be happy with the performance of its pension fund this year.

What about the perspective of fairness? Isn't the aim of prohibiting insider trading to make the markets fairer for participants who wouldn't customarily have access to privileged information? And hasn't one of those participants just been given a little instant fairness? It's hard to imagine a more deserving bunch of tippees.

We start to run into trouble when we examine the rights of those involved. When it comes to market matters, there's a strong argument that we ought to think of everyone involved, all the time. Admittedly, there's no reason to suspect that the Special Schools pension fund has done better at the *expense* of another investor. But it's still done better. What gives Colavito the privilege to choose who will benefit at all? And what if everyone acted the way she has?

On Absolutes

Are there overriding ethical principles that should govern our actions regardless of the effects of those actions considered in terms of workability and fairness? If so, who gets to decide what they are?

Consider again the hypothetical African oil field we visited in Chapter 2. Some people would argue that the company responsible for wounding the land should take steps to heal those hurts, regardless of short-term cost or the opinions of local residents. Such advocates champion the concept of humanity's stewardship of the environment. The earth is entitled to protection. Each individual company has an interest in profit. But *all* companies, it is argued, have a common, "transcendent" interest in preserving and protecting the planet's general health and dwindling resources. And this is true regardless of the short-term human sensibilities involved.

Since approximately four o'clock in the afternoon of October 24, 1929, the day America's wildest bull market started to stumble, policymakers in this country have generally subscribed to the "transcendent ethic" that participants in the securities markets ought to behave in a way that justifies public confidence in those markets. Manipulation is bad, and corporate information should be available on an equal basis to anyone who cares to ask. This "transparency" helps the solvency of the specialist on the floor of the exchange. It also helps keep the market orderly, which in turn bolsters the confidence of investors.

Still, critics often point out that other countries have managed to build strong markets despite the fact that regulators there are more lenient with regard to insider trading. Maybe the reason we try to keep our markets straight comes down less to analysis of stock pricing models than to ideas we hold about ourselves as a nation. These are ideas of fairness, the melting pot, and the level playing field— notions like the one that a Pakistani immigrant ought to have access to the same sorts of information about the market as a Boston Brahmin. The stock market, in other words, is one more place where we transact the business of being American, with all its sloppy inconsistencies and dogged high intent. With this in mind, perhaps it's easier to swallow the idea that the market itself is owed some respect. That those of us who participate in it professionally, whether as corporate execs or financial analysts, are in a way the *market's* fiduciaries.

At least that's the theory. Reality has a few holes in it. It's common knowledge that insiders make dirty money every day. Would discovering this be enough to change your convictions, as it may have changed Colavito's? Would you be willing to pass information, whether for immediate profit or to cleanse your conscience, if you saw others doing it too?

One of the biggest challenges of working in the financial markets is maintaining a commitment to fairness when you know not everyone shares it. Colavito's tip to her favorite client may be *de minimis* in the sweep of history, but it sets in motion a pattern of privilege and cover-up that can, in the long run, harm her employer and corrupt Colavito's judgment. In this sense, maybe her small and arguably "just" action *is* unpragmatic: for Coyne Portfolio Services, for the markets in which it operates, and for Mary Colavito herself.

Control Time

Even the dullest stocks were paying 12 percent by the end of 1928: an excellent rate of return, better than you might get by putting your firm's capital into further production. Not only that, the price of shares themselves was going up. It was irresistible. No work, no skill were required; there was no chance (it seemed) of losing.

Hugh Brogan
The Penguin History of
the United States of America

Chapter 5

Granada's Golden Years:
The Dangers of Following
Accepted Wisdom (1989)

It is financial professionals who have the greatest
obligation to resist investment fads. It's our job to
lean against the wind of the moment.

Periodically the market starts to gallop, intrigued by tulips in Holland, land schemes in Florida, stocks or bonds, genomes or chips. Investors go bouncing along, shrieking like Sooners, and even the soberest analyst can find himself mesmerized by the short-term rates of return a given gold mine produces at the height of the hysteria. The problem is that short-term gold mines can turn into long-range gutters. It's a question of timing. A matter of months. Or sometimes of minutes.

A well-meaning man named Philip Granada found himself captivated by a particularly alluring financial product of the 1980s and discovered that success can be as paralyzing as failure. Here's his story:

Maybe you're wondering how I ended up down here. I wonder myself, sometimes. I was in my 30s and had been practicing corporate law in Atlanta for six years when the four of us—me, my friend Andy Bean over at First Financial, and two of his bond trader friends from Jacksonville—put our heads together and decided we were ready to start our own business. We fixed on the financial industry because deregulation seemed to be opening everything up in the field. From the start, Andy and I were the day-to-day guys. The Jacksonville boys threw in plenty, but they were content with a percentage of the take, and left the details to us. The stock market was struggling with high interest rates, and we couldn't finance a new brokerage firm with ourselves as the only customers. What if we'd started churning the accounts? That's a joke. But we figured a dreary old savings bank with a decent customer base might be just the sort of operation we were looking for. The feds had recently stepped up the insurance guarantees on individual accounts, and the state legislature had given the green light for S & Ls to invest in just about anything they cared to, including real estate.

In 1983, we found the perfect opportunity down in Jolene. Stewart Savings was a tired old neigh-borhood-mortgage bank owned by a couple of 60-year-old brothers who were the first people I'd ever met who actually enjoyed whittling. They were getting pretty good at it, too. Had a lot of practice, since their depositors' cash was flying out the door for money market mutual funds that paid double the bank's rate.

I won't bore you with the details of our negotiations. Andy was our numbers man. In the end we bought out the Stewarts with bonds backed by the assets of their own bank, reserving the right to call those bonds at a premium if we were successful in moving the operation into high gear. That meant, besides the fact that the Stewart Brothers probably shouldn't have been in the financial industry in the first place, that we could spend our own capital on building the business.

A quick survey of our depositors showed that most of them were card-carrying members of the local Social Security set. Not the best demographic if you're trying to sell basketball shoes, but it did give us something to build on. We bought a list of the names and phone numbers of everyone in the county over the age of 50 and hired a couple of marketing people to start making cold calls. Changed the name of the bank to Golden Years Savings & Loan and started handing out a plaque to every 25-year depositor. Every time we handed out a plaque, we made sure the local rag was on hand to take photos. Lots of photos. We really leaned on our old-fashioned image.

Our growth strategy, on the other hand, was completely up-to-date. First thing we did was bite the bullet and sell all our outstanding low-interest home loans to a mortgage bank at .70 on the dollar. (We'd taken the loss into account in our deal with the Fabulous Furry Stewart Brothers.) With the proceeds, we invested in 10 percent short-term paper. We aimed to run ourselves like a money-market mutual fund, promising our depositors the highest returns in the region.

Our research showed that older folks appreciate personal service and it was okay with them if they had to stand in line a few minutes to get to the teller. They didn't *want* to use the cash machines. They enjoyed the chance to chat with their neighbors, with the tellers, with the security guy who used to deliver their newspaper and always threw it into the azaleas— whatever. So while other banks stressed automated banking and deposits by mail, we decided that sort of time-is-money, get-me-to-the-Stairmaster-and-hand-me-a-cappuccino stuff only made sense for busy working people. Our market was different. We took our local experience and built a franchise network, always keeping our eyes open for other savings banks that might be amenable to joining up. Soon we had affiliates in Arkansas, Alabama, and Texas. That's how we got to be The Golden Age Network for Savings: Service With a Smile.

Eventually, through Andy, who knew a couple of the head guys, we struck up a relationship with Counter Securities, a pipe-rack broker out in L.A. that was making a niche for itself in the high-yield market. We worked out a joint venture in which we agreed to supply Counter's customers with high-end government-guaranteed CDs in return for Counter supplying us with the bonds to *fuel* those CDs. Seemed like a real win/win proposition.

Of course we offered our bank customers similar rates. It was revolutionary. Beautiful. Appalling. Here are these retired old geezers, used to poking along at a 6 percent return, suddenly looking at 15, 16 percent interest a year. We couldn't beat 'em off with a cane. And I felt good about it. You know, if some old schoolteacher tells you she thinks she can afford to fly down to Aruba this year instead of just schlepping over to Pensacola because she's making an extra three grand a year on her money market account, you think, hey, I must be doing *something* right.

It wasn't long till a lot of other brokers got into the high-yield act and the junk market went white-hot. Suddenly it wasn't just Michael Milken pushing the stuff—everybody was selling it. But we couldn't expect any of the big guys to provide the special synergy we had with Counter, and synergy was a big part of why we were doing so well. So we stuck with Counter to pick the issues and pretty much bought what they recommended.

Lobbying was my department. I took on the title General Counsel and started to meet with the regulators. Met with them. Lunched with them. Even *hired* a few of them eventually.

Congressmen were the same only different. We played golf in Pro-Am tournaments, took the occasional fishing junket out in the Gulf. Not that the marlin were worried. These were social trips, mainly. A few beers. A few bucks. Eventually I agreed to serve on a couple of state re-election committees, and gave money to this PAC or that one. Whatever. The affiliations weren't important. It was the people that counted. Getting to *know* those people, and making sure they knew me. I was representing our banks, and the holding company and, practically speaking, Counter Securities—which picked up most of my expenses.

It was around this time—1986, I guess—when Andy started getting nervous about our investment tactics. Said he was losing faith in the high-yield market, and came to me a couple of times with the suggestion that we start easing out of bonds. Maybe I should have listened harder. But the market was wired, right? I figured we had to keep going, make the bucks while we could. I wasn't stupid. I'd know when it was time to get out. It was all a question of time. And anyway, I was starting to feel like, even if the market *did* roll over, we'd come out all right. We'd gotten in pretty tight with the government folks and if everything collapsed, so what? No way Congress was going to let retirees start eating dog food. They'd do *something*. Tax money would cover it.

When I said that, Andy just stared at me. I said *what?* and he came back with some lecture about what we'd set out to accomplish with Golden Years. I said we'd set out to get bigger. And we *were* getting bigger. On some lists we were one of the 10 most profitable S&Ls in the country. It just didn't look like it was going to end. So much for Andy. He sold his stock. And I noticed he didn't have any trouble getting the price he wanted.

Anyway, at the height of the market, we created a service company to manage the back office and marketing materials for the CD distributions of our affiliates. They paid us a fee based on our success, and we provided the mailing packages. That was when we started pushing the slogan "Never Lost a Penny," emblazoned on a rainbow above an old tintype of the Stewart Brothers' bank. We went cyber, too, sending laser disks to our affiliates for show-and-tell to customers while they were waiting in line, along with floppies to help their local marketing people merge their mailing lists with our letters and envelopes. The local TV ads said, "Remember: No Depositor at Golden Years Ever Lost a Penny."

I guess we'd have to amend that now. The bubble burst and for awhile you couldn't give junk bonds away. Golden Years started bleeding money. One quarter. Then two, and three, getting worse as our bond portfolio went belly-up. We had some bad luck with our real estate holdings, too, which made matters that much worse. So much for diversification. We ended up broke. Bankrupt. Whatever you want to call it. The media got into the act, and there was a run on the bank, you might say. Like to have seen Jimmy Stewart stop *this* one.

It all ended up pretty much like I figured it would. The federal government stepped in, and in the end most folks came out okay. (Not that I'm a big fan of the federal government, mind you. Too much waste. Too little faith in the common man.)

Of course there's still some people in Jolene I wouldn't want to meet up with in a dark alley, but hey—they can read. They should have figured there might be some inconveniences along the way. And as you probably know, I spent some time in a federal facility. *Which* facility doesn't matter. Let's just say it wasn't the Library of Congress. I lost my airplane, my condos, even my Jag. But my wife stuck by me, and things are looking better now. Thanks to the Homestead Act, I was able to keep the house down in Florida, and I'm back on my feet. Run this charter-boat service out of Fort Lauderdale on my 32-footer, the *Charles Colson*. I try not to do business with any politicians, though. Too many memories.

Reaction:

_____

_____

_____

_____

_____

_____

_____

_____

_____

_____

Debits

Seeing as how Golden Years Savings & Loan no longer exists and Philip Granada hints at having spent some time in the pokey, it may not be necessary for us to wonder if his actions as head of a briefly thriving bank were "pragmatic," in the enlightened sense of the term discussed in Chapter 2. The one practical thing he and his high-flying brethren accomplished for their investors was drawing federal officials into such close complicity with their financial shenanigans that those officials were later required to pledge U.S. monies to resurrect ruined banks like Golden Years. Unfortunately, this was also one of the least *just* things he did, at least from the point of view of the much-abused American taxpayer, who is still in the process of paying the billions of dollars needed to clean up the mess that men like Philip Granada made of the savings and loan industry.

It's easy to blame Granada because he failed to see the end of the '80s high-yield bubble. But the fact is, market expansions of the junk-bond variety are extremely hard to resist. Investors in the 1920s rode a rising ocean of equities for years, piling up unheard-of profits. When that sea finally turned, wiping out a large part of an entire generation's savings, America gained the enduring image of stockbrokers falling like strange fruit from the concrete orchards of Wall Street.

Despite the temptations, it's financial professionals who have the greatest obligation to resist investment fads, can't-miss deals, pressured sales. It's our job to lean against the wind of the moment. To question commercial wisdom. To doubt our own best guesses. The broker or banker can eat all the sea kelp he wants. Track flying saucers. Read Madam Blavatsky. When it comes to the money entrusted to him by others, he has to stop chasing chances. Was this duty even greater for Philip Granada, who knew from the start that his bank's clientele consisted primarily of elderly people? Was he acting with due respect for their interests by plowing the bank's funds into speculative instruments and ADC loans, even when these investments seemed a sure bet?

Granada says at one point that his clients were happy with what he was doing for them. Are there situations in which a financial professional ought to *disregard* what a client wants? And was this one of those situations? Or, if financial professionals can continue to count on the United States Treasury to cover their stupidity, do such questions even matter?

Get the Facts

Derivatives can give you enough
leverage to blow yourself up.

Robert Gumerlock
Swiss Bank Corporation

Chapter 6

Derivative Dreams:
A Risk by Any Other Name (1995)

Appealing to a buyer's vanity is perhaps the oldest sales technique on record. For a financial professional, this vanity is primarily intellectual.

Derivatives get no respect. The casual newspaper reader can easily get the impression that these mysterious instruments bear toxins capable of wilting the strongest cerebellum and breaking even bricklike banks. In fact, though, derivative instruments are morally neutral, and possessed of an ancient and rather unsalacious history. The generic *derivative* is simply a contract whose return is "derived" from another source. This source can be a commodity or currency, an index or interest rate—just about anything an investor cares to imagine.

Small Potatoes

The primary use of derivatives has traditionally been to *hedge*, or insure against, volatility in the price of a commodity. Agriculturalists have traded derivatives for years. Say a farmer grows nothing but potatoes. It looks like he's going to have a fine year and, if prices hold true to form, he'll realize 12 cents a pound on his crop. On the other hand, he well remembers what happened two years ago, when a bizarre fungus broke out in numerous potato shipments and liquefied thousands of tons of Idaho spuds. FDA warnings to consumers resulted in widespread panic, a congressional inquiry, and a rash of UFO sightings in the skies over New Jersey.

Needless to say, demand collapsed. Potato prices plummeted.

If our farmer wants to protect himself against a repeat of the potato fungus disaster, he might try to sell part of his crop before it's ready for market. Maybe he can't get 12 cents today for a crop that won't be ready for another three months. But let's say Drug Frontiers, a Minneapolis-based pharmaceutical firm, is extremely high on potatoes because its scientists have discovered that potato oil stimulates hair growth. Drug Frontiers needs all the potatoes it can get to carry on its heady research, and is willing to pay the sodbuster 10 cents a pound immediately for 4000 pounds of tubers meeting contract specifications, delivery three months from today. If he accepts the deal, our farmer has hedged against the possibility that potato prices will drop below 10 cents a pound. Meanwhile, the pharmaceutical firm can put 10 cents into its budget confidently.

Simple enough, right? But here's a wrinkle. What if our farmer contracts to sell his potatoes to a middleman—a commodities trader? Assume the farmer gets the same deal. What's different here is that the trader has no personal use for the crop, and has entered the trade to make a profit. She's heard some interesting rumors on the street and, drawing on her sense of the almost inexhaustible vanity of the human male, is edging into the potato market. Here she's purchased a *derivative* contract. She's paid $400 today in return for whatever two tons of potatoes are worth three months in the future. Assume the rumors are correct. Potato oil does stimulate hair growth, even in chihuahuas. Once word gets out, the per-pound price of potatoes rises overnight to 50 cents. The commodities trader has spent $400 for the right to a crop that is now, only three months later, worth $2,000.

The Swap

Suppose one additional fact. What if conditions point to a bumper year for soybeans? And what if our sodbuster is willing to take, instead of cash, a contract for delivery of soybeans three months from now? Assume that in return for his potatoes, the commodities trader gives the farmer a contract for 2 tons of soybeans at 10 cents a pound, to be delivered in 90 days. Knowing that soybean prices are famously stable and that soybeans have in fact sold for an average of 12 cents a pound for the previous several years, the farmer happily accepts the bargain.

In this case, both the farmer and the trader have acquired contracts whose worth derives from the value of their referenced assets. They've simply swapped risks—and "swaps" are an important genus of derivative contract. The farmer has swapped to protect himself from a swing in the price of his main crop. The commodities trader has swapped a stable asset for what she hopes will be an asset that fluctuates wildly—*up* being the preferred direction.

Deals like this are done every day. Banks swap interest rates. Multinational corporations swap *currency* rates. When done thoughtfully, derivative contracts can reduce risk and guarantee income streams. Despite their frequent usefulness, however, derivatives can be dangerous in a couple of different ways.

Playing With Fire

First, derivatives, like any other financial instrument, can be bought on margin. Look at our potato example again. Suppose that instead of simply paying for a single potato contract up front, either with cash or a contract swap, our commodities trader buys numerous potato contracts on margin. She doesn't pay $400 dollars today for the right to own 4,000 pounds of potatoes three months from now, with the possibility of a measly $1600 profit. Instead, she gives our farmer $80 as a sort of downpayment to guarantee delivery of those 2 tons of potatoes at ten cents a pound in 90 days.

The trader then does the same thing with four *other* farmers. She has now spent her $400 in return for delivery of 10 tons of potatoes three months in the future. If potatoes are worth 50 cents a pound at that point, she's made a great deal: the crops she contracted to buy for $400 are now worth $10,000. But if the potato market has crashed and tubers ˙ℯ going for 5 cents a pound, our trader owes $2000 for ˙ℴes she may be able to sell for a total of only $1,000. she increased her potential profit by buying on margin, she also increased her potential for loss. This, brutally simplified, is how people lose big money on derivatives.

A second danger in dealing with derivatives is that they can be extremely complicated, limited not so much by human ingenuity as by microprocessing capacities. Computers understand them fine. For the rest of us, it takes some work. And in some cases, this work is not being done.

Ignorance in the financial marketplace is rarely as obvious as that of the state financial official, identified in the *New York Times*, who didn't know that parentheses around certain figures on an accountant's spreadsheet meant that those figures were losses and who bragged of his mid-day meetings with Wall Street's "Stanley Morgan."

Still, misunderstandings are rife in today's markets. In contrast with the law, where people are constantly asking each other exactly what they mean (sometimes to ridiculous extremes), financial professionals often nod their heads and pretend to comprehend the math or the market. It's bad enough when a potential investor doesn't follow the deal. It's worse when the salesman pitching it doesn't either. The situation is deteriorating as financial products become more sophisticated and the calculations behind those products more complicated. There are now securities whose prices are tied to the performance of an index, securities whose prices are tied *inversely* to the performance of an index, index swaps, pools of mortgages with variable rates tied to interest rate indexes, and various other options and instruments that require a graduate degree in mathematics to be fully understood.

Advances Leading Declines?

The driving force in all such innovations is, of course, money. First and foremost, the innovating firm wants greater profits on its trading activities. Second, it wants an edge in the competition to be reported in Lipper or Morningstar as #1 in yield, in total return, or in capital performance. Even momentary preeminence can encourage a parade of enthusiastic new customers, many of whom fail or forget to understand that higher potential yield implies higher actual risk.

Inevitably, some supposedly sophisticated investors, investors who should understand this relationship a little better, have also been burned by innovative instruments allowing for ever-more aggressive leverage and speculation. A man named Robert Citron was a widely admired public servant who traded securities and derivatives for the investment pool of California's Orange County. The harder it got for him to make a buck, the more he borrowed. Mr. Citron's bet was on interest rates not going up. When he lost, the bill came to billions of dollars. The debt actually forced the county into bankruptcy. Mr. Citron abruptly retired in 1994, explaining that the fault for his crap-out lay largely with his broker/advisors.

Gupta's Big Move

It was in the aftermath of Orange County's crash that Sanjay Gupta, a 33 year-old Indian money manager, got his first big career opportunity—an opportunity he's only recently begun to regret. Here's his story:

I earned my master's degree in Finance at INSEAD, then spent several years charting interest rate trends for Seaborne Boston. Eventually I was promoted to manage short-term reserves for Seaborne's family of mutual funds. And felt like I was set for life.

Three years later I was ready for bigger things. And I had a friend, Regine, who knew I was getting bored in Boston. One day she called to tell me the brass at her company, Magnesse, were looking to "retire" the manager of their Dollar Account Fund in favor of someone younger and more aggressive. Regine started the ball rolling by forwarding my resume to the Hiring Committee. They weren't too put off about my work experience being exclusively in the U.S. since I'd gone to Europe and had to speak fluent French to get into INSEAD. It turned out my credentials made a nice match with the position. And I must say that during my initial interview I talked a good game about running pooled funds.

In leafing through the file they gave me, I found that Magnesse's portfolio of U.S. dollar and Eurodollar bonds wasn't really being managed at all. My predecessor had for years bought a ladder of bonds going out 20 years, with a fraction maturing every six months. He was basically operating the way bank trust departments used to invest before customers began to complain about paying them lawyers' rates for being able to multiply and divide.

So I explained that if Magnesse hired me, my primary goal would be to increase yield. I could tell they were still a little antsy, so I suggested leaving 65% of the portfolio, all the longer bonds, intact. I would take the short-end bonds, the other 35%, and manage the hell out of them, though I'd still keep the credits at AAA—mostly U.S. Treasuries and agencies. Average maturity of the new portfolio would be three years or less. I'd consider moving into some variable-interest rate paper as well.

That seemed to cinch the deal. We shook hands all around and I went downstairs to pick up my security card. I gave myself 100 days to turn the fund around. I knew I'd be pretty much on my own out there. I didn't have a lot of time to prove myself, and in my first week made a lot of sales, putting the money into one- to four-year maturities. I kept the average maturity for my portfolio at about two years to keep my boss, Charles LeMaitre, calm.

A month later I felt the looks when people passed me in the hallway and knew I had to do something to increase returns. Regine suggested maybe I should call an old classmate of hers named Janko Kirkby, who does what he calls Risk Management Control at Metropolitan First in Chicago. I called Janko and told him that I had to get my yields up quick. Like, yesterday. He said he had some ideas and thought he could structure a note to meet my needs.

We met in a conference room at O'Hare. Janko brought an overhead projector and a couple of support staff from the Bank. He'd heard about me from Regine, he said. Impressive credentials. And speaking of impressive. Janko Kirkby looked like he wrote the book. I don't know what book, exactly. Maybe the Armani catalogue.

But all he could talk about was how far I'd come, and how young I was to be running a fund for Magnesse. He said it was clear I knew what I was doing, so he'd skip the introduction, which was for someone he called "Bushers". He flashed various topics up on the screen and said I should just ask for more details if I thought he'd skipped something. He suggested that I think of the generic presentation as a sort of checklist, with my job being to state specifically what I wanted at the end. Then he'd make some phone calls to figure out the exact numbers we could get.

The presentation was over in ten minutes. Janko shut off the projector, and we sat down to hammer out the deal. I wanted a top credit issuing the paper. No problem, said Janko. We would deal with Fanny Mae, the Federal National Mortgage Association. There would be supporting derivative contracts, but the note would be issued by FNMA itself. Full faith and credit, right? Our principal wouldn't be at risk.

I wanted liquidity.
Again, no problem. Government agencies were among the largest issuers of these structured notes, giving them a good source of borrowing at an attractive cost. It was a deep market, in the trillions

of dollars. The note would be structured with the FNMA commitment to paying us interest every three months.

I wanted a three-year maturity.
Done, said Janko.

I wanted to receive a higher-than-market rate of interest.
Okay. We'd begin with a very high coupon rate with later coupons variable, increasing or decreasing as a public index increased or decreased. Because of the ready availability of quotes, the index Janko recommended was the London 3-month rate (LIBOR), then running at 3%. That was agreeable to Fanny Mae.

Janko put all this together and the initial coupon came to 8%, believe it or not. We discussed how that could be done, which I'll explain in a minute. But for me the most important point was that we had a AAA credit and our return could never go to a negative figure: we'd never have to pay anything back.

My fund was at $450 million. I was managing 150 of that, with $300 million still tied up in the ladder bonds. I signed on for a $25 million FNMA note, structured as Janko had described it.

Here's the FNMA promissory note as described in my worksheet that day:

DOLLAR ACCOUNT FUND
Borrower—FNMA
U.S. $25 million par
Repayment—3 years
Interest rate variable
Starting coupon 8%—see #1 below
Interest rate index—3-month LIBOR

1. *Formula: current interest payment equals 11%*
   minus current LIBOR index rate. As the index
   rate is currently 3%, the arithmetic is simple.
   11% - 3% = 8% per annum.

2. *Risks. Repayment of principal in 3 years;*
   virtually no risk, given that FNMA is the
   borrower.

Interest rates will vary. But we'll start well above
current levels. Disregarding some minor expenses,
this is the math:

<u>*11% minus differing rates*</u>
11% - 1% = 10%
11% - 2% = 9%
11% - 3% = 8%
11% - 4% = 7%
11% - 5% = 6%
11% - 6% = 5%
11% - 7% = 4%
11% - 8% = 3%
11% - 9% = 2%
11% - 10% = 1%
11% - 11% = 0%

Unless the index is pushed to 8%, we'll be doing better than if I bought a plain vanilla 3-year FNMA note. I don't see the Fed tightening rates by more than a couple of points, if that. I like the odds. Even with a doomsday scenario, if LIBOR goes to 15%, we don't have to pay them for "negative" income. We can't get less than zero. Janko said there's a side-deal cap in the package, a sort of insurance policy that will cost us about 1/2 of 1%.

3. *As long as interest rates stay steady or drop, we get 8% or more from a AAA credit. If we want to sell the note before the three years are up, there's a very liquid market, with bids available in a matter of minutes.*

4. *Janko earns his money by turning what FNMA wants to pay (which is whatever LIBOR is) into what we want to receive, which is a floating rate that starts higher than current interest rates. His job is to get rid of the variables like the ups and downs of the interest rate index, which FNMA doesn't want to deal with. The bridgemakers he hires are swap and option traders.*

As I see it, if we hang on till the end of the term, Janko's work will be of academic interest only. We have a contract to be paid interest quarterly and principal in three years by FNMA. We won't have to look to anyone else.

***

On the flight back to New York, I scratched out a few more notes to myself. I guess I was preparing for the day when I might have to explain the whole thing. I wrote:

The Steps

• Fannie Mae wants to borrow at a conventional rate and is agreeable to paying the three-month LIBOR figure, including its fluctuation up and down.

• My Dollar Account is willing to accept an index-related payment but wants a rate well above market.

• Janko agrees with FNMA to take the three-month LIBOR rate payment and to come up with the money to accommodate us. His business is simply to put together a deal in which he doesn't take the risks of future changes in interest rates.

As the first step in developing the braces for his bridge, he needs to get rid of the fluctuating payments he's going to receive from FNMA—to swap them for a fixed amount. He gets a bid from a swap trader to pay 5 1/2 % a year in return for the FNMA variable commitment. Under the formula, Janko has to pay us (by way of FNMA) 11% minus the LIBOR interest rate (so he's exposed to the LIBOR index rate fluctuations on the payment side) and needs to swap that variable also for a fixed payment. The bid from the swap broker is (logically) also 5.5% for that payment. Neat. Now we know where the 11% comes from: the two swap transactions. Janko knew what the structure of the deal would be. He got the two 5.5% swaps and slid their costs in as the first item in the formula.

• Is Janko at risk? What we receive can't exceed 11% even if the LIBOR rate index rate drops to zero. And if LIBOR goes up to 15%? 11% - 15% = -4%. But as part of the deal, our minimum income is zero. And Janko has a commitment he bought from an options dealer for 1/2 of 1%, where the dealer will put into the pot any "negative" income arising if LIBOR exceeds 11%.

• These swaps have been arranged by Janko to protect his bank, of course. But they're essential to the deal and are transferred to us as part of the structured note, so that we have the advantage of any benefit.

***

At first the deal worked like magic. The 3-month LIBOR rate seemed to have found its equilibrium at 3% per annum and we were getting our 8% interest every three months. I explained all this to LeMaitre, of course, but he went glassy-eyed when I started talking about deducting the LIBOR rate from 11% and drawing Issuer and Swap Trader boxes on the blackboard. He understood that 8% was more than 3% and that the portfolio as a whole was up, but beyond that he wasn't impressed.

After six months, I added a second $25 million three-year note with similar terms. And after six months more with market rates holding steady, I added a third note. By then I had the attention of the team. I had $75 million earning 8% in a 3% market. With a U.S. credit, to boot. Damn right I had their attention.

I'd told them that if interest rates went up, we would get less on our notes, but they just shook their heads and smiled. They gave me a couple of assistants and a window office. I bought a Porsche. Which was tempting fate, I guess. The Fed started to tighten credit, and rates rose to 4%, then a few days later to 4½. The yield on our notes dropped.

A month later I flew back to Chicago to see Janko Kirkby again. Word on the street had it that interest rates were going to keep climbing. I wanted to become more liquid. I'd established my firepower at the firm by now and didn't need the extra yield to keep my job. I told Janko, in fact, that I was interested in selling the notes. The pricing service we used for the fund valued the notes at around 97 on the dollar. I could live with a 3 point loss.

Janko said that price sounded optimistic to him, and called a couple of his own brokers for a quote. One bid 90 1/2, the other 90 1/4. I thought he must have the wrong CUSIP number, but he shook his head and said something like, "You have a problem with that pricing agent. He doesn't realize these are FNMA structured notes and sell in a separate market.

You told me three years was a short time and you had plenty of liquidity in the fund. This is a very marketable security, but the value of a structured note is determined by looking at the whole picture, specifically at the market value of your two swap contracts. You yourself see the Fed goosing up rates."

He added: You know all this, of course.

Of course, I said. And he said, "Then the problem for you is simply finding a way to explain it to your boss." Which was right on the mark. I could see where Charles LeMaitre might have a big problem with why the bid for our particular notes had dropped so much more than the market generally. I might have to explain it for him in a way he could understand. Like with little stick figures or something.

Look, I could say. This security is not like a stock that may never come back. It has a fixed maturity at par and a AAA credit rating. It's the U.S. Government, for God's sake. To which he'd reply, "Then it should be safer, no?"

I went for a walk around the concourse. Bought my sister Rupa a Cubs cap, had a cup of coffee and came back to see what we could do. Janko and his grunts had been cranking away. Looked like they'd been through meetings like this before. Janko and I sat down across a stained table and hammered out my dwindling options.

1. I could stand pat. Let the notes mature at par. But my interest return might sink to zero in the meantime.

2. I had a bid. Bids last about ten minutes if you're lucky. So should I sell the notes? And do what with the $67 million?

3. I could keep the notes and do some hedges through Janko or someone to protect against further erosion, recognizing that what's lost is lost. In effect, I might unwind part of the transaction, selling the risk of further rises in interest rates. On the other hand, I wouldn't be dealing with AAA credits in that market and I'd have to walk with my hands out in front of me.

4. I could rework the portfolio as a whole. Sell the longer and high-risk instruments? But I'd told Charles LeMaitre I wouldn't *touch* those bonds. Increase credit quality? Maybe I could shift the proceeds of bonds that are maturing to short-term Treasuries until I had more of a handle on what to expect of interest rates.

5. I could sound the alarm. Janko told me I needed to get the big dogs (that was his way of saying my boss) in on the act. They needed to know they had a problem. Easy for *him* to say.

6. I could throw myself into a bonfire. Waste whatever karma I've managed to accumulate over the centuries, come back to Earth as a lobster or

fruit bat and never have to worry about index rates again.

But it wasn't so bad. On the trip back to New York, I reminded myself that I had achieved what I'd set as a goal. I had increased income for the fund. Current income was over market, and I hadn't lost a cent of capital.

If the pricing service was correct, if the Fed held off on further tightening, I would still be in good shape. The first note was halfway to being paid off at par. Even the third note was only three years from pay-off. I'd play this close to the vest and see if I could make a little money for the Fund by trading short-term Treasuries. I'd get one of my assistants working on reducing administrative and brokerage costs and the other one on ways of increasing income, like finding soft dollars to pay custodial fees and earning fees for our lending bond certificates.

I think I'll survive this one. I know that derivatives have a bad name because they've been abused and managers have taken risks their funds couldn't afford. My God. Leeson playing with billion dollar chips like a kid in a neighborhood poker game. I took some risk, and if it had been in researched-small-company equities there would have been disappointment but no persecution. Here, I have a great credit and I'm betting we'll come out better for taking the high-yield initial coupon under the terms of the note. My sister Rupa tied that stupid string around my wrist on *rakhi*. Now I'm glad she did. Not that I think some string's really going to protect me from all the evil out there, but hey—I can use all the help I can get. I'm going to stand pat, as they say. As if I had a choice.

Reaction:

_____

_____

_____

_____

_____

_____

_____

_____

_____

_____

_____

_____

_____

_____

Bullshitting for Fun and Profit

Let's cut to the chase: There's no way Sanjay Gupta could have been acting ethically in any of the three respects we've discussed if he didn't fully understand the notes he bought from Metropolitan First. Judging from his reactions to Kirkby's pricing quote, Gupta was more than a little confused. And what makes his story interesting isn't trying to figure out what segment of the transaction he didn't quite get but pondering how frequently these days all of us are, in effect, Sanjay Gupta.

It doesn't matter which side of the deal you're on. Purchasers of derivative instruments are taking their complaints to court fairly frequently these days. As the *New York Times* observed of a lawsuit in which the state of West Virginia claims to have been misled by Wall Street investment bankers, "hundreds of similar [actions] are just being filed—cases in which low-paid and, often, poorly trained state employees say greedy brokers led them astray with securities they did not understand." It's the old story: Evil Suits Fleece Virtuous Bumpkins.

But the last decade has seen a curious turn, in which financial professionals are fleecing themselves by buying into investments they only pretend to comprehend. Some observers treat the situation as comedy. In *Bombardiers*, for example, Po Bronson speaks of Wall Street's "bastard language, the illegitimate offspring of technical financial terminology and forty years of pop Americana, littered with ill-chosen metaphors and living acronyms."

One of the bonds Bronson's salespeople are assigned to flog is designed to jump start investment in post-communist Romania. The Romanian bonds, we learn, "had an average duration and an implicit call option and a single monthly mortality and a dollar-weighted return," none of which the young traders really fathom. But one of the baffled bombardiers nevertheless "rattled the phrases off with sincere confidence, and her customer, Mike Kohanomoku at Honolulu Federal Savings, didn't want to admit to her that he had slept through his graduate school lectures on fixed-income securities. He pretended he understood completely."

Or More Seriously

Other observers have attempted to explain the phenomenon. In a 1991 article for the *Yale Law Journal*, Professor Henry T.C. Hu of the University of Texas School of Law analyzes exactly why so many financial professionals, and the regulators charged with overseeing them, are finding themselves behind the knowledge curve with respect to modern financial instruments. How is it, he asks, that "banks suffer from such systematic informational failures?... How could such knowledgeable *sellers*, as opposed to investors or consumers, not have adequate information?"

According to Hu, there are several reasons. One has to do with the concept of *appropriability*, an idea borrowed from scientific research and development. Simply stated, appropriability in the securities context means the ability of the originator of a financial formula to make exclusive use of that formula. In the financial world, where such formulae generally cannot be protected by intellectual property laws, appropriability is very low. One bank's product is bound to show up across the street almost as soon as it proves profitable. Thus, the originating bank has big incentives for prompt and massive marketing, but much less incentive for extensive research about the possible failings of a given product.

Another, less abstract reason for the information failure involves the damnably lucrative nature of some derivatives. Derivatives traders at a given bank may simply find it convenient to understate to their superiors the extent of the risks the traders are incurring with their transactions. Nicely anticipating Nicholas Leeson's destruction of Barings Bank in 1995, Hu states that the temptation to downplay the risks involved with one's activities "is further exacerbated by the extraordinary asymmetry in payoffs. In the event a trader is caught, he may, at most, lose his job and suffer reputational losses. On the other hand, a successful gamble could mean lifetime wealth."

Janko Kirkby seems to understand the deal he's sold to Sanjay Gupta. Can you see how he might have overcome Gupta's reluctance to enter a transaction he (Gupta) only vaguely comprehended? The appeal to vanity is perhaps the oldest sales technique on record. For a financial professional, the vanity is intellectual. No one wants to look like he doesn't understand the situation. Kirkby plays on this weakness. "You understand," he says—implying, *hey, your bosses might not get it, but we do, right?*

Cut out the b-school jargon and it's basically the same scam they use down at Crazy Al's Auto Emporium. "You look like someone who knows a little something about cars," says the salesman. "Whatta ya think of this baby?"

There are probably two sensible ways to react in this situation. The first, of course, is to run like a dog. The other, possibly more difficult, is to answer truthfully: "Fact is, I don't know a thing about this particular car. Suppose you start talking—slowly—while I take a few notes."

Chapter 7

Digging Deeper:
How Much Diligence is Due?
(1994)

*Or are there some principles, some beliefs, that ought
to override all considerations of pragmatism and
cultural deference?*

Not everything can be modeled. Knowledge in the
financial professions is still a matter of comprehending
not only the details of a particular deal but also the character
of the people who are doing it, and—in some circumstances—
why they are doing it. As American business and banking
personnel fan out around the world, from Bangkok to
Bucharest, they are encountering situations they may not
have covered in their college classrooms. One financial
professional, Liliane Chen, an attorney with a white-shoe
New York City law firm, tells her story.

I don't think I'm a hero. Just the opposite, really. I'm actually an idiot. In this instance, I just happened to be a sober idiot.

My personal life isn't terribly relevant to much of this. But if you insist: I grew up in rural Virginia, not far from D.C. My parents were immigrants from Taiwan. Engineers. And both of them, as it turned out, took jobs with the federal government. I suppose they thought living in the boonies was going to be good for us kids. I hated it, though. We were the only Chinese people within like, twenty miles. The other kids said we looked like frogs. Threw bricks at my brother. I couldn't wait to leave for college. Couldn't wait to prove myself. You're not supposed to say this, but I felt superior to those jerks I grew up with. And you're not supposed to say this, either: I still do.

At Harvard I just wanted to be like everyone else. I listened to the same music, took the same drugs. I even dated a hockey player. And I used to sell chocolate chip cookies from a little cart at the edge of Boston Common. Like any other good American kid, I graduated with no plan for what I wanted to do next. Be an artist? A writer? A magician's assistant? Eventually I hired on with a consulting firm in Washington and, after a couple of years of that, went off to law school at Yale. Harvard. Yale. Only the best, right? I suppose I got that from my parents. When you're an immigrant, the names are important.

I took a job out of law school with Wakeman &
Taft, the most arrogant and prestigious firm I could
find. They actually laughed when I asked how many
associates made partner each year. I had to respect
that kind of snottiness. Sure, I worked 70 hours a
week, but what the hell? I'd already proved I wasn't
Picasso. I'd have been wasting my time if I wasn't
working, and the work was the best around. At
Wakeman you don't just start out in a field and stay
there for the rest of your career. You rotate every
year and a half, so you can learn corporate law from
several different angles. I did M&A (overrated),
some Bankruptcy (hated it), and a good deal of project
finance.

A year ago the firm decided it wanted to open up an
office in Hong Kong. It wasn't a terribly original
thought. In fact, the primary reason for establishing
the office was that so many of the big investment
banks, and so many of the other law firms that *service*
those banks—Davis, Polk, Sullivan & Cromwell,
Brown & Wood—had already showed up in Hong
Kong. I think Wakeman was beginning to get a
little nervous about getting cut out of the Chinese
Renaissance.

Which is exactly what it is, a renaissance. The
Chinese in Singapore and Hong Kong and Malaysia
control incredible amounts of wealth these days, and
they're using it to drag drab old China into the 20th
Century. Investing everywhere, in just about
everything, from infrastructure to underwear.

When Wakeman asked for volunteers to open the Hong Kong office, I surprised myself by signing up. I'd always been skeptical of ethnic nostalgia, and I hadn't even practiced my Mandarin since I was a kid, but as soon as I heard about the office I wanted to be there. Turns out I was the only associate to volunteer; they had to assign three others to fill out the team. Dalton Marrs, who was about two years away from retirement, and Ken Rippey, who'd just made partner the previous year, were put in charge of the office.

I'll spare you the travelogue. I ended up living in a nice place in Midlevels, just above Hong Kong's Central District and a five-minute walk from the office. With Wakeman's reputation and close ties to American banks, we started to get business almost as soon as we opened up. Most of it was pretty bland—I suffered through three months on a series of aircraft financing deals, for example—but in November I started working with Ken on Eight Dragons.

Eight Dragons is an expatriate Chinese conglomerate with a finger in just about every commercial activity you can imagine. Michael Wu, the so-called Sultan of Singapore, calls the shots, but it was originally funded as a sort of joint investment company operating with funds donated by the heads of eight prominent families in Malaysia, the Philippines, and Taiwan. Eight, right? The Chinese lucky number. If you know anything about the way Chinese do business, you know that the actual capital donated by these eight families was a lot less important than the connections—the *guanxi*—they brought to the table. Michael Wu never had to look for investment opportunities. He usually had to fight them off.

I'm not sure why Eight Dragons decided it was time to raise money in the U.S. Maybe it was vanity. Maybe they felt like it was time they announced themselves to the world, though generally that's a very un-Chinese thing to do. Maybe it was a sort of invitation to the Chinese in America to start looking East with their money. There's always been a sort of "gathering" instinct among the expatriate Chinese. It's not widely spoken of, but even in my hardheaded family there was this feeling that China was still the place where it all began and the irreplaceable source of, I don't know, *Chinese*-ness. I know it's not a word. But there's definitely this loyalty, and it's gotten people in trouble before. Back in the '50s, when Mao was still arguably sane, he called out to Chinese expatriates, particularly Chinese in the West, to return home and help build the glorious new People's Republic. A lot of Chinese Americans were stupid enough to go. What they ended up building was a lot of glorious new Chinese prisons.

Eight Dragons was interested in spinning off a division to raise American dollars to support and expand its manufacturing operations in China. Originally they went to Rosen Merritt, our investment banking client, and announced that the funds raised would be spent on whatever Eight Dragons felt like spending it on. Dave Gentry, the lead banker at

Rosen Merritt, promptly delivered the first of his many perorations on U.S. securities law and its detailed disclosure requirements. Michael Wu and his colleagues were appalled to find out, then and at about a dozen meetings afterward, just how much information the SEC was going to require in connection with an equity offering. We worked for about six months with Rosen Merritt and Eight Dragons in figuring out how to structure this new division, how to define its capacities, and trying to trace out its place in the Eight Dragons network, which was this absolutely stunning and—to an outsider—completely unintelligible web of interlocking investments, informal partnerships, and controlling interests.

Eventually we figured out a way to isolate a piece of the network. We called it Dragon Communications, Inc., and defined its purpose as the manufacture of consumer electronics, which we figured would appeal to the American market. This was also a field that Dave Gentry and his number crunchers felt Eight Dragons could do quite well in. They'd established excellent connections with national and provincial authorities in Wuhan and Guilin, who'd pretty much given them carte blanche to build the sort of manufacturing facilities they wanted. Labor was dirt cheap, and a lot of the components were being manufactured in China already—which meant that even the hardware was going to be inexpensive. Amazingly inexpensive, really. We were all excited about the prospects.

As the senior associate on the deal, I was responsible for performing the due diligence investigation. Ordinarily that's a real yawner of an assignment, but in this case, it turned out to be fairly interesting. Due diligence in the States can mean anything from pawing through the last ten years of corporate minutes to reviewing 300-page labor contracts. In China it tends to mean something like, "You say you've got a factory? Prove it." And they did. I jumped on a series of South China Airways flights and found myself in places I couldn't even locate on a map. I was treated like a visiting celebrity. Given the grand tour, treated to meals of owl soup and bull's penis, complimented on my halting Mandarin.

Actually, it was my Mandarin that caused the trouble. On my last tour, of a telephone manufacturing facility in Wuhan, we started what turned out to be a nine-course meal at about seven o'clock. By eight-thirty my translator for the day, a morose little man named Li Wang, was so drunk that he couldn't locate his glasses, which were perched on his nose. We'd entered the congratulatory phase by now, and I managed to make some kind of lame toast about how amazed I was at the low costs associated with manufacturing in the country and how the hard-working Chinese were going to out-compete the rest of the world and sell a billion telephones.

When I'd finished, Li Wang said something like, "Of course they're hard-working."

And I said, *What?*

And he said, "Of course they're hard-working. What else is there to do in prison? Sing karaoke?"

In half a second, I was sober.

I said, *What do you mean? Who's in prison?* But I knew already. There was one part of the assembly line I'd never seen. I'd asked. No one had answered. It was where the phones were actually put together. You know—snapped and glued and screwed together. And suddenly it hit me. Of course I hadn't seen that. No one was going to see that.

"What prison?" I said.

But Li Wang had sobered up, too. And everyone at the table was staring at us. The plant director. Two provincial officials. My host from Eight Dragons. The room was silent. Like a tomb, or something. It was undoubtedly the most uncomfortable two minutes I've ever spent. But I know one thing—Li Wang felt a hell of a lot worse. And I've never seen him since.

The rest is complicated. Of course I told Dalton and Ken what I'd heard at the banquet, and what I'd come to suspect about exactly why Eight Dragons was able to achieve such wonderful economies in the manufacturing process. Ken was like, *so what?* He said Wall Street isn't Disney World. We take on clients just as we choose, regardless of how popular or winsome they are. But Dalton shook his head. He understood my concerns. He said everyone remembers Tiananmen. If the Chinese government isn't as ecstatic about the importance of individual rights as we are, fine. But doing the legal work on a U.S. equity offering that would be backed up in part by concentration camp labor was beyond even Wakeman's tolerance levels.

Dalton was in touch with the New York office. They came back with the edict that we either get Eight Dragons to change its labor arrangements or drop out of the deal. Easy enough, right? But when we went over to the offices of Rosen Merritt to let them know what the firm had decided, Dave Gentry went ballistic. He said it was none of our (read: *my*) goddamned business how the company made its products and anyway how could I know for sure and did we know how arrogant we were to go applying Western ideas to a people who'd been civilized for thousands of years before Europeans even learned to put on pants. He had a whole set of permutations on the theme of cultural relativism, but I figured it all boiled down to one of the oldest philosophical justifications: Money smells stronger than sweat. Rosen Merritt stood to make millions selling the deal in the States, and hoped to do a lot more business with Eight Dragons.

Dalton Marrs said, Dave, do the deal if you want to. But unless Michael Wu cares to change his production methods, we're out.

Gentry was livid. Said if one word got out about this, he'd have Wakeman Taft's ass for breach of attorney-client confidentiality rules and when the other banks on the street heard about it we'd have to start using our corporate expertise on McDonald's *franchise* agreements because no one wanted to work with a bunch of goddamned priests and if goddamned Wakeman was going to start kowtowing to the reservations of a two-bit associate, maybe it was time Rosen Merritt started reviewing some of its business allocation policies.

That was my cue. I stood up and looked at Dave Gentry and saw every arrogant name-calling selfish bastard I'd ever known in Fairfax County and ever after. I said, "Mr. Gentry, I think I'd like to excuse myself now. Because you're making me sick. You want to underwrite something?" I lifted one finger. "Underwrite this."

And I walked out.

Dalton hasn't stopped laughing to this day. I may make partner at Wakeman yet.

Reaction:

_____

_____

_____

_____

_____

_____

_____

_____

_____

_____

_____

_____

_____

Meet the New Boss; Same as the Old Boss

There's not much more we can say about Dave Gentry's actions here that Liliane Chen hasn't already said better. But what about Chen herself? Was she right to blow the whistle? Did she go too far? Has she gone far enough?

In this connection it is important to know that attorneys are subject to their own broad set of ethical guidelines, originally promulgated by the American Bar Association and subsequently adopted, in one of two forms, by bar officials in all the states. The ABA Model Rules of Professional Conduct forbid an attorney to disclose potentially damaging information about a client unless the attorney believes the client intends to inflict serious bodily harm on another person. The "transcendent ethic" here is that people should be encouraged to seek out the advice of counsel and be able to trust that what they say will not be repeated. Given this ethic and the rules that derive from it, the only real option left to Wakeman Taft is to withdraw, silently, from its representation of Rosen Merritt. Or is it?

How can we appraise Liliane Chen's insistence that her employer rethink its involvement in the Eight Dragons deal? Let's start from the perspective of justice. Chen has clearly made a "just" decision here—one concerned with doing right for other people. Whether this decision will turn out to be pragmatic for her and for her employer is a little less obvious. Maybe the firm will lose business—from Gentry's bank, if no one else.

But how good could it be for a firm to participate knowingly in exploitation of prison labor? There are obvious PR risks. But can't we go a little deeper? What would it do to the people involved? This means the prisoners, of course. Their lives probably won't improve much as a result of increased demand for their services. It also means the lawyers at Wakeman Taft. Is there anything degrading in taking advantage of other people's helplessness? And what if the PR risk could be eliminated? What if Chen and Marrs could be certain no one would ever find out about the prison labor? Would it be okay to go ahead with the deal at this point?

Dave Gentry suggests that Chen ought to have a little more respect for the rights of her client's client, the Eight Dragons organization, and its mainland Chinese partners. If they want to use prison labor, why shouldn't they be able to? The Chinese don't have to share Western beliefs in order to make good trading partners, do they? Or are there some principles, some beliefs, that ought to override considerations of pragmatism and cultural deference? If so, which of your beliefs are that important?

Consult

I'm sorry.

Nicholas Leeson

Chapter 8

"Trust Me":
On Consultation and Captaincy
(1990)

In attempting to hoist Mayflower into her own conception of the modern financial world, Elsa Gutierrez has quite blithely ignored—worse, failed even to see—a host of possible ethical problems.

American culture exalts the gunslinger in us all. We're loners, deerslayers, pioneer scouts. It's a difficult picture to do without. Yet the modern financial markets, with their endless acres of information and legions of godless bushwackers, are remarkably poor prairies to ride alone.

It's easy to understand why companies might want their employees to share information. What's less often extracted from the cases of modern-day mavericks like Nicholas Leeson, Joseph Jett, and Toshihide Iguchi is the conclusion that consultation might have prolonged *their* careers—that, in other words, they would have benefited from seeking out supervision just as much as their employers would have benefited from giving it. From some exchange of ideas. From someone occasionally saying, "Mind telling me what exactly it is you're doing?"

Elsa Explains It All for You

Consider the case of Elsa Gutierrez, an ambitious and extremely capable Latina from McAllen, Texas. After graduating from Swarthmore, Gutierrez joined the corporate loan department of a medium-sized bank and trust company called Mayflower. She brought investment banking insights that had not previously been available to Mayflower, and within six months of her hiring helped to restructure and save two important customer relationships for the bank. In light of her quick successes in the loan department, she was identified as a potential member of senior management and given an early promotion to vice-president, with a roving assignment to trouble areas.

At Gutierrez's suggestion a long-term planning committee, reporting directly to Mayflower's President, was established. Gutierrez was named secretary of the committee and, at its first meeting, asked to focus on the lagging revenues and increasing expenses of Mayflower's trust department, which had come to be a major concern of the bank's chief financial officer. Because salaries were not competitive with those of independent investment managers, good people were leaving the bank. Poor portfolio performance discouraged new business, and profits in the department were marginal or nonexistent.

Looking back on her assignment, Gutierrez recalls that the solution seemed clear:

Cutting through the fancy packaging, the job of the trust department had always been to attract and retain upscale banking customers. Where I differed in my approach was in insisting that the bank's products and services had to be tested by how profitable they were. Even the tired old trust department had to be justified by the bottom line. Otherwise, we might as well have sold it off.

Of course I was never exactly *in* the trust department, I was more a liaison between top management and the staff over there. I brought a fresh look, a new perspective, to a group of employees who had gotten a little too self-satisfied. My understanding was that it was my job to get Mayflower's trust department up to speed, and that I had official backing for that job.

A lot of these trust types were still living back in the 1970s, when performance was ignored and service was everything. They were nice enough people, well-educated and all, but they were gun-shy and it was costly for the bank. Our customers were growing increasingly performance-oriented at a time when our investment record in the department was about as flat as Nebraska. This affected customer confidence in the main show, on the commercial side. It was a cancer we had to cut out, and cut out right away.

What a mismatch: a big staff and a lot of small trusts, each of which was administered separately. A rich guy died, his taxes were paid, and the rest was split up into half a dozen separate trusts. The smaller the account, the more painful our fixed costs were.

My goal was to consolidate, to get the assets of the individual trusts into a common trust fund of some sort. I know all about that "personal service" crap. What it boiled down to was some trust officer taking a widow to lunch at the club and maybe mentioning the stock market in between aspics. My way, we'd have a single person making the investment decisions. Hopefully, we could build up enough transaction volume to get some attention from the brokerage houses—get their ideas on hot stocks for the trust department and lock up their customer-loan business for the bank. As for the widows, we could serve tea at 3:30 and see them there. Iced tea. In styrofoam cups.

I figured our first priority would be to take the common fund and build up a second quartile investment record we could advertise. That way we could make a profit on the small trusts and at the same time start attracting some larger accounts. In one sense, my work in the personal trust area was just a prelude. After all, the money's not in the personal area these days. The really big fees are in pension trusts.

Success in marketing by itself wouldn't guarantee us any profits; I knew we were also going to have to change our system. As we added more accounts, we were going to have to add new software and more specialized marketing and client relations people, especially in the pension area. There would have to be some change in personnel, too, which was a major reason why a lot of the old crocks were dragging their feet from the very beginning. After all, they weren't stupid. They knew some of them weren't going to make it. I heard they started calling me "Alligatierrez." *Cabrones*. They were shivering in their wingtips.

Well, you can read all about my plans if you want to. Here. They're all in this report. And it looked like they were going to happen, too. For awhile.

You've heard the expression "blindsided"? That's what happened to me. Guy by the name of Charlie Noteboom was head of the Trust Department. Always seemed friendly, always had a smile. Never exactly agreed with my ideas, but never wanted to argue about them, either.

I remember once he asked me to lunch. We sat and ate soup and he sort of pondered out loud, like he was Socrates or something. You know, talking about how I saw the trust relationship as "retention selling" of a bank product, but that trained fiduciaries—*like himself, of course*—were skeptical of the notion that all trusts should be treated uniformly and dumped into a common trust fund, regardless of its performance and the differing individual investment objectives or needs of the beneficiaries.

He said he and his colleagues were also uncomfortable with increasing the volume of the small trusts' securities transactions, because of the very result that I saw as attractive. In my mind, more brokerage transactions generated more commissions, more commissions meant more research from the brokers, and more research from the brokers meant reduced research costs for the bank—and of course better performance for the trusts. All Charlie could think about was that the customer was going to have to pay twice for management, through both brokerage and trustee commissions.

I don't know. Sounded to me like he was just rambling. I had a securities professor like that back at Swarthmore. No one paid any attention to him, either.

Turns out quiet Charlie went straight to the Board of Directors. Said he didn't like what was happening to his department, and was planning to leave Mayflower if my recommendations were accepted. Said I hadn't even bothered to get his view of the situation, that I didn't know what I was doing, didn't understand the nature of the fiduciary relationship, *etc., etc.* Three other Trust Department people turned in letters of protest at the same time, along with—and this was the killer—nine *clients*, who threatened to raise holy hell if I had their money dumped into some sort of pooled fund. I don't know what they thought we were going to do with it. Buy junk bonds? Go to Las Vegas?

The whole thing just snowballed. As soon as the other pringles in the Trust Department saw what was happening, they jumped on Noteboom's wagon and threatened to resign as well. Folks at the bank started giving me funny looks. I got an angry letter from a longtime trust customer.

Well, you can probably guess what happened next. The President wasn't about to put his butt on the line. He asked me if I wouldn't mind a sort of re-assignment, and stuck me back in the loan department for awhile. Meantime, he was going to appoint a three-man committee—with Noteboom the chairman—to study what to do about making the Trust Department more profitable.

Funny thing is, they ended up using a lot of my suggestions. Of course I didn't think it was funny at the time. I was mailing out resumes. But maybe it all worked out for the best. I'm doing fine, now, back where I feel like I belong. Here in South Texas, where the only snakes you have to watch out for rattle their tails before they strike.

Reaction:

_____

_____

_____

_____

_____

_____

_____

_____

_____

_____

_____

_____

_____

Trusts and Fiduciaries

Fiduciaries are trained to look at the different interests created by a trust and to treat each appropriately. The typical personal trust involves one party entitled to current income (the "income beneficiary") and a charity, child, or relative entitled to the capital when the income beneficiary dies. Fiduciaries have a duty to safeguard the funds under their care as if those funds were their own. In this case, it was only natural for them to question Gutierrez's pressure to consolidate the small trusts into a pooled fund that could be managed more aggressively. True, Gutierrez sees how the pool might increase returns for the trusts involved. But there would be a price for the individual trusts as well, because they would have to bear the increased commission costs and capital gains taxes.

Gutierrez mentions better investment performance, but achieving better performance is tricky. In general, performance can be increased legitimately only by employing better (i.e., costlier) investment professionals, decreasing diversification, selecting stocks with higher volatility, and/ or looking at shorter-term horizons. Since Gutierrez doesn't refer to hiring better investment personnel, the only available tools may involve increased risk.

La Cuenta

The alert reader will see in this case a reverse image of Chapter 3, in which Rusty Merrick led his bank into battle as the trust department waved peace signs on the sidelines. Here, it's the trust department that triumphs. Common to both cases, though, is the tension between the bank as fiduciary and the bank as market participant. This tension will only increase as Congress pulls down the last bricks of the Glass-Steagall Act and commercial banks are freed once more to invest pretty much as they please. Their self-restraint, or lack of it, will be one of the central issues in finance for the next decade.

Is this case really about ethics? Or is it about politics? Elsa Gutierrez would like to see it as the latter: she, a sort of latter-day Joan of the earnings arc, has been burned by her short-sighted enemies within Mayflower Bank. She was, after all, only trying to help. She sees her actions as pragmatic. The bank and its shareholders will benefit from the increased profits she hopes to create. She's doing justice as well, since she's trying to increase earnings for Mayflower's shareholders and the trust beneficiaries—who certainly, from her perspective at least, have a right to aggressive investment management and the robust returns such management may produce.

Still, even Gutierrez's very cursory rendering of Charles Noteboom's complaints suggests that Noteboom may have had legitimate worries. Is he right to worry about the effects of plans to modernize Mayflower's trust fund earning objectives? Of course. Is he right to subvert these objectives? We don't know. More importantly, *Gutierrez* doesn't know. She's talked, but she hasn't listened. Consulting with even the Nootebooms of the world ought to be treated as more than a matter of courtesy. It ought to be recognized for what it is, a drop-dead vital ingredient of responsible decision-making.

The result? In attempting to hoist Mayflower into her own conception of the modern financial world, Elsa Gutierrez has quite blithely ignored—worse, failed even to see—a host of possible ethical problems. And is acting this way ever really pragmatic?

Chapter 9

Whose Vote?
Co-opting the Consultation Process
(1987)

*Can you see long-term problems if a senior executive
is allowed to sway a committee of independents on
issues in which the bank has a financial interest?*

We often talk in absolute terms of shareholders as the
owners of a corporation, and ritualize their annual
meeting as the quintessential expression of participatory
management. But in modern finance, even ownership is no
longer simple. In fact, ownership can best be seen as a
bundle of rights—possession, management, the ability to
sell or give away—often held by different people.

The profile of shareholders in major U.S. corporations
has changed radically in the past few decades. In the 1930s,
political scientists Adolph Berle and Gardiner Means wrote
of a policy vacuum created by concentration of company
ownership in the hands of passive individual shareholders—

we'll call them "the filthy rich"—many of whom had inherited control stock from entrepreneurial ancestors. This policy vacuum was filled by corporate managers, who did pretty much as they pleased.

These days, institutional shareholders are dominant. They have access to a breadth of information and are, at least when it comes to trading, extremely active. But for antitrust, financial, regulatory, efficiency, and political reasons, institutional investors and their intermediaries have been reluctant to play more than a spectator's role in the affairs of the corporations in which they invest. Political activists see lethargy in such inaction, or even a deliberate abdication of fiduciary responsibility. However, these activists might complain even louder if they thought bank trustees and other professional intermediaries were intervening for improper reasons.

Attack of the Gadflies

Criticism of institutional inertia is most often directed at the practice of routinely endorsing corporate management proposals at annual shareholders' meetings. In the 1950s, so-called "corporate gadflies" (they were called plenty of other things as well) like the Gilbert Brothers, Wilma Soss, and Evelyn Davis began to joust with the management teams of various publicly-held corporations. One thing they pushed for was cumulative voting rights—rights that would enable a minority of shareholders to cast all of its votes for a single nominee and thus acquire minority representation on boards of directors.

Corporate gadflies backed other radical proposals as well. They called for *preemptive* rights that would allow shareholders to purchase new issues of a company's securities before the public, thus allowing those shareholders to preserve their proportional influence in corporate voting. And they demanded that the location of annual meetings be shifted around the country, to increase communication between shareholders and management.

Seems tame enough now. At the time, though, these proposals tended to be automatically rejected by the various street name nominees, both banks and brokers, who were comfortable with the "Wall Street Rule" on proxy voting: SUPPORT MANAGEMENT OR SELL THE STOCK. One rationale for the Rule was that if each issue had to be voted on after a thoughtful review, the result would be expensive and chaotic. Delays might occur because of a lack of quorum for the necessary meeting, and a subsequent remailing by the corporation would be needed to resolicit the shareholders in order to *achieve* a quorum. And all this would occur when the outcome of a given vote was probably a foregone conclusion anyway.

Socrates Never Wore Suspenders

The game changed when headline issues—issues that had little bearing on the day-to-day business of a corporation but impinged on the public policy attitudes of many institutional investors—began to be presented for discussion. Trade unions pressed the managers of their pension funds to invest in labor-friendly firms. Church organizations tried to block drug companies from foisting pharmaceuticals on unsophisticated Third World consumers, and environmentalists demanded that Gaia be given a voice in the way natural resources are consumed.

Such issues resist the rationale of the Wall Street Rule. They can't easily be quantified and given a dollar cost and benefit. With this in mind, it might seem to be ethically overreaching for an institution to cast its customers' votes on such proposals at all. Ideally, the votes would come directly from the beneficial owners themselves. But that's rarely practical. Proxies generally arrive three or four weeks before a stockholders' meeting takes place. They go to the owner of record, often the bank's or broker's street name nominee. After the bank's own analysts review the proxy and look at the business issues, only a few days remain to return the proxy to the corporation. If the client is a pooled fund (a pension trust, a mutual fund, *etc.*) and one wishes the ultimate investors to express their views on a social responsibility issue, the communication and mechanical problems involved are virtually insurmountable.

Deciding Who Decides

Issues concerning the governing machinery of corporations may seem to be more straightforward than those involving environmental and ethical claims. But governance issues can be equally complex and have both financial and social side effects. Which brings us to our case. Consider the following response from Douglas Dalton, a trust officer at Cleveland's Cuyahoga Trust Company, concerning his employer's success in formalizing consultation procedures on "social issue" proxy votes:

> I'm happy to talk about ethics and how I vote our proxies. Of course it isn't really my full-time job. My main responsibility is trust administration.

Here on the personal-trust side of the bank we do the voting ourselves. It used to be routine. You just stamped the card and sent it back. Sometimes an officer would take the proxy cards along to the annual meeting so he could make some brownie points with the portfolio company. You know. Show 'em how big the bank's holdings were, so he would have a leg up in seeing a senior officer the next time he wanted to pitch a new product. But all our holdings are public information now, required by the S.E.C., so we just mail in our proxies like everyone else.

When the Gilbert Brothers were active, the proxies didn't bother us. If you didn't like management, you sold your stock. Otherwise you kept your trap shut. After all, what's the point of investing in a management team unless you're going to support their workaday decisions?

Then suddenly political issues were coming in from everywhere. It started during Vietnam, when the peaceniks wanted Dow to stop making napalm so the U.S. Army would have a tougher time turning Southeast Asia into a giant parking lot. When Dow ignored them, the activists went to the S.E.C. in an attempt to get their demands on the agenda of the stockholders' meeting. When the *S.E.C.* turned them down, they went to court. They got some congress-men all stirred up on the issue, too. Eventually the S.E.C. staff came up with a formula: if the proposal was tied into the business of the target company—for example, by being framed as a proposed charter change or a mandated report to the shareholders—

the proposal would be deemed appropriate for the shareholders' meeting despite the opposition of management. Abstract propositions, on the other hand, would not.

Of course, after Vietnam all sorts of political issues showed up on the proxy ballots. There were proposals to ban the use of nuclear energy, to block companies from doing business in South Africa, to prohibit firms from accepting defense contracts. Eventually the right-wingers got in on the act with their own set of issues, like cutting off all sales to the Soviets. Not that the conservative issues ever got really big. It just shows that a lot of this stuff was politically motivated, rather than having much to do with business *per se*.

The corporations were obviously interested in getting our votes. We expected that. More surprising was our discovery that some of these second-generation gadflies and their supporters were customers of ours who seemed more interested in social issues than in how well their stock performed. Over in the corporate trust department, where we had college endowment-fund customers, the problem became a major priority. Which they naturally punted to us.

These issues don't lend themselves to financial analysis. It's more a matter of sociology or—again—*politics*. Whenever there was a news story about a corporation having a squabble with the community, you could bet there would be a resolution on the subject at the spring shareholders' meeting.

So there we were. We couldn't shift the responsibility to one of our number crunchers, and we couldn't vote in favor of management across the board. Not without running the risk of losing some of our own customers. And finally, what with all those trusts, we couldn't just run a quick poll of the beneficiaries every time a vote came up. Wouldn't be practical.

Eventually the bank decided to set up a committee and pass the buck on social issues to *it*. I was named chairman, and assigned to think the deep thoughts with Joanna Buckley, a Sociology professor from Penn State, and Ned Levine, a political writer. You may have seen Ned doing those PBS debates with Bill Moyers. You know. "Is the Heart an Overrated Organ?" and "What's the Matter with Malthus? He's All Right!" Joanna tends to lean to the left. Ned comes across as a Neanderthal on the air but is actually pretty sensible in person. Neither one actually knows a junk bond from a jackboot, so I take the lead in explaining any of the tangential business issues we run into. And I'm a moderate, so we've got a pretty good balance.

Here's the way it works. If I think a proposal might have a significant *financial* impact on the company involved, I vote the proxy myself, checking with anyone in the bank who could be helpful. All other proposals go straight to the committee. For example, even on South African questions I used to call one of our research analysts to find out the profit and loss implications for, say, X Company's South African operations. Usually they were minimal and the issue went to the committee.

Or maybe a better example would be the cost to an aerospace company if it were to be prohibited from doing business with the Defense Department: that would be right at the heart of the company's earnings projections, and I would vote the proxy myself. Anyway, with the nonfinancial issues, the social issues, I outline the shareholder proposal and my recommendation in a memo to my writer and my professor. They agree or disagree and that's that— a majority vote carries unless one of us asks for a meeting on it. We meet three or four times a year anyway, just to go over how the proxy season is unfolding.

The system works pretty much the way we hoped it would. If the bank has a customer who disagrees with how we vote, we're able to explain our system of committee independence. And if some company is knocking our door down, lobbying hard, our CEO agrees that the committee will look at any materials the company cares to provide. It's a lot better than any other system we've been able to think of.

There's another benefit to the committee format. Though we welcome any and all submissions of information, we tell everyone who asks us to side with them that the process is entirely confidential and we won't divulge the way any one of us as individuals actually voted.

Here's a checklist I've developed. I answer the questions as best I can and circulate it to the committee for every shareholders' meeting that has contested issues on the agenda:

1. *Significance to the company.* How expensive would it be for the company to comply with the resolution? For example, does the resolution say that the company ought to abandon a plant? Or is the proposal simply to report to the public data that are already available internally and easily transposed? Even here we have to be careful that the company isn't being asked to give up confidential information that might hurt its competitiveness.

2. *Harm; to whom and how much.* What harm is being claimed? For example, on the use of nuclear power, is there any risk to a nearby community?

3. *Who's proposing the resolution?* Is it a believable shareholder with a significant stake in the company and the company's performance, or just some crank with a handful of shares looking for publicity?

4. *How will the bank's customers be affected?* What have we heard from them? And will there be a specific effect on our own community? For example, an issue might not cost the company very much money overall, but could have a large effect on the bank's customers and on the bank itself.

We get help with the details on all these issues through a proxy service in Washington called the Investor Responsibility Research Center. The I.R.R.C. spells out the opposing arguments on an issue and provides whatever documentation we need. Each committee member gets a set of materials, and it helps to have this reasonably objective back-up to look at when some partisan pushes hard.

Recently we've started seeing new sorts of proposals in addition to the social issues. These are the so-called corporate governance questions. For instance, should female directors be required? Should every board have a union representative? Or a person, such as an academic, who doesn't have *any* ties to the company? Should a majority of the directors be outsiders? Should there be a *nominating committee* made up of outsiders? In a sense, these are like the old Gilbert Brothers issues, but they come from both sides: management teams are also pushing a lot of governance points in order to protect their companies from unfriendly takeovers or to ensure continuity of management.

In fact, we're considering a governance issue now. It's what the M&A people call a "shark repellent." The management of Forth Right Financial is proposing to create a new holding company in Delaware that would acquire the business of Forth Right. Delaware law permits a company to limit the rights and powers of its shareholders more than other states, and the new Delaware holding company would promptly issue preferred stock that would have the power to veto a merger or acquisition.

The problem is, our customers hold a fair amount of Forth Right stock and Stanley Nguyen, our analyst, is mumbling about lost takeover opportunities if we vote Yes. He agrees, though, that Forth Right has good managers who have done well by the shareholders. Earnings have increased steadily and the stock is up nine points in the last two years.

Here's part of the actual proposal:

> *REORGANIZATION PLAN—Approve a plan that would make Forth Right Financial a wholly owned subsidiary of a new Delaware company, Forth Right Inc. All shares of outstanding stock of the operating company would be exchanged for equivalent shares of the holding company stock. Forth Right Financial will remain an Ohio corporation. The reorganization facilitates future expansion and diversification of business activities because the holding company structure will afford a broader choice of financing and organizational approaches.*

> *We also have entered into agreements with 15 of our key executives that provide for the following payments in the event that any of the executives is dismissed within 36 months after a change in the control of the company: (1) accrued vacation pay; (2) between two and five times, as determined by the board, the executive's highest annual base salary; (3) between two and five times, as determined*

by the board, the executive's highest incentive compensation paid during any one of the five years immediately before the change in control. In addition, upon a change in control, bonuses pending under the company's management bonus plan and awards of stock under the incentive stock option plan would vest immediately. Stock options also would be exercisable immediately upon the change in control.

We propose a new stock option plan to grant key employees incentive and nonqualifying stock options. The company would make available 4 million shares of common stock for the plan. Option prices would be no less than market price at the time of the grant. There are about 300,000 outstanding unexercised options under the existing plan and no new option grants will be made under that plan. The company has approximately 20 million shares of common stock outstanding.

Going down the checklist I mentioned earlier:

Significance cuts both ways. These new provisions can help a good company protect itself. You can't really quantify what the takeover opportunities are.

Harm. The harm seems remote. The sponsor is a responsible management team.

Cost. Management says the costs are reasonable.

The bank's customers. Forth Right isn't a customer of the bank, at least not yet, but I got a call today from Jay Rostropovich in our business development office with the news that the company is now a pension fund prospect. *A really big pension fund prospect*, Jay said. More than once. Can't blame him for the excitement, though. We haven't had much new business like that for a while.

It isn't as though there's anything illegal about which way you vote on any of this. In fact, if you think it through, the long-term shareholder who wants to stay with Forth Right is probably not served very well by an unfriendly acquisition. So I've recommended that we vote for management in this situation. Get this Delaware thing taken care of. My memo will be simple to write—all I have to do is look at the points the I.R.R.C. views as favorable.

Something like 15 shareholder proposals concerning different companies arrived on my desk this week. Using my checklist, I'll probably be able to get the whole package out today and get back to work. So you can see how our system encourages prompt, ethical decision making.

Reaction:

_____

_____

_____

_____

_____

_____

_____

_____

_____

_____

_____

_____

Voting on the Committee

Everyone deals with conflicts of interest. Think of such occasionally divergent loyalties as God and country, career and family, desire and duty. Yet we balance our own allegiances in a workable way every day without much discomfort. As managers, we also routinely balance the conflicting claims of those affected by our decisions. But we should look twice when an intuitive conclusion supports our self-interest. Are we really just rationalizing a conclusion we've already reached in our own favor?

Before deploying our three perspectives on Frederick Dalton's decision, let's focus first on his employer. What do you think of the Cuyahoga Trust Company's committee approach to questions of social responsibility? We might question what the qualifications of the committee members should be, but the mix here makes sense—and the committee could, of course, add an outside resource person when that seems useful. In any event, the simple efficiency of the current plan is admirable.

Voting on Dalton

What about Dalton's actions? Given that Cuyahoga's committee is a good attempt at institutionalizing the process of consultation on difficult questions, is Dalton acting pragmatically by abusing this process? In the short run, his influence on the Forth Right vote isn't going to kill the committee. But can you see long-term problems if a senior executive is allowed to sway a committee of supposed independents on issues in which the bank has a financial interest?

The beneficiaries of Cuyahoga trusts who own Forth Right stock rely on the experience and disinterestedness of Cuyahoga for protection. It's their shares the bank is voting. Is Dalton's behavior *fair* to these beneficiaries? He seems confident that the beneficiaries won't suffer at all from a vote in favor of Forth Right management. But we don't know whether this proposal is actually a last-minute change blocking an imminent tender offer. All else being equal, it's hard to see why a bank that functions as a trustee would develop a sentimental attachment to a stock whose upside price may be artificially limited. Common sense suggests that corporate management tends to take this type of action only when a practical benefit (*viz.*, blocking an unfriendly assault) is in sight.

And are Dalton's actions fair to Buckley and Levine, who may well have come to trust their committee chair's motives? Consensus among experts can only work if there's an open dialogue. In this case, the new business pressure may well have warped Dalton's judgment. Whether the pressure is self-generated or comes from someone higher up in the management of Forth Right may not matter. This sort of influence can be very hard for any employee to sort out and discount. By participating in the proxy decision, Dalton is manipulating his committee. There is probably a base of goodwill built up that gives Dalton's views a special weight. Under these circumstances, however, his views should in fact be given *less* weight than usual.

Assuming he would like to, how could Doug Dalton improve the impartiality of his committee? In this case, should he disclose the prospective relationship between the bank and Forth Right? Is this enough? Would it be better for Dalton to abstain altogether, admitting that a conflict exists without implying in which direction the conflict would prompt the bank? What would *you* do if you were in Dalton's place?

Bowing Out

A more fundamental question is whether the committee as constituted is even competent to review corporate governance issues. Unlike most social responsibility questions, governance issues like this *can* significantly affect the value, price, and marketability of a company's stock. As they require financial analysis, such issues are more within the body of professional expertise of a securities analyst than of a sociologist. It may, however, be unrealistic to expect Stanley Nguyen, the Cuyahoga analyst assigned to Forth Right, to be trained to evaluate the proposed preferred and the move to Delaware, both specifically and as a precedent for other situations.

If he can't shift the responsibility to a trained analyst, Dalton remains the key figure. Maybe Nguyen could prepare a memorandum for the other members of the committee. To ask him for information at this late date could be tricky unless the request is limited to a list of pros and cons rather than a recommendation. Of course, Nguyen is also subject to the same sorts of pressures—another friendly call from Jay Rostropovich?—that Dalton faces.

Maybe a rule that states "abstain where there is a relationship," or even the possibility of a relationship, should apply to both Dalton and Nguyen. Such a rule would help preserve the impartiality of the process, and in turn allow consultation to do what it's best at—exposing the decision-maker to new voices and different, possibly valuable, perspectives.

Identify Those at Risk

Am I my brother's keeper?

Genesis 4:9

Chapter 10

Rooting for the Home Team:
Where Do We Draw the Line? (1995)

*It's only human to conclude that our neighbor is the
good guy and the out-of-towner an adversary.*

Getting a fix on the possible consequences of an action
involves many of the steps we've already examined.
For example, the decision-maker should already have
considered the distortions of judgment her own interest in a
situation may cause. She ought to have studied the facts,
factored in—and tried to *relieve*—the time pressures on her
decision, and consulted with those who could help her in
the process. With these steps completed, she can start to
focus on the point of all such exercises: figuring out how
other people will be affected.

One Evening on the Internet

Tender offers pose tricky problems for everyone involved. Only a few of the issues are quantifiable, and even they generally involve projections rather than facts. Ask Rosalind MacReed. Ms. MacReed has for several years been one of Prescient Portfolio Services' top managers. Her current priority as a fiduciary is the Salaried Employees Retirement Trust of the M. L. Retton Co., Inc., a local sporting goods company and one of Prescient's most important clients.

MacReed isn't making billion-dollar trades or threatening the solvency of a sovereign state, but she is on a rather hot seat. Retton has recently come into play at the hands of The Motley Group, a midwestern conglomerate. In considering the issues this takeover bid has presented to her and to Prescient, MacReed has called upon one of her oldest friends and, through the magic of e-mail, downloaded her doubts on U.C.L.A. Finance professor Daisy Chan. We pick up the exchange in mid-transmission.

...as a senior vice-president I'm gradually moving out of day-to-day management, but I've still got a couple of funds to worry about. The most interesting at the moment is the M.L. Retton retirement fund. I don't know if our takeover fight has shown up in the L.A. papers (I kind of doubt it, we're not that big), but it's keeping us pretty busy here in Ohio.

We've managed to put up some good numbers for Retton over the years and we have a terrific relationship with the people over at the company. My Retton counterpart tends to get promoted after about two years supervising the fund. As a result, I've had several bosses who are now V.P.s but used to be in the controller's office and dealt with me in connection with the mechanics of the fund—actuarial assumption changes, funding requirements, new wrinkles added to the pension plan, *etc*. I mention this just to show that I'm in a fairly good position to help them with the Motley Group bid.

I don't know exactly what's been going on in the boardrooms over at Retton. They seem calm enough. No matter what a target company says, though, a takeover bid has got to be rough on management. Just before the Motley request for Retton shareholders to tender their stock hit the papers, Retton stock was selling at $42 a share and earning $7 a share. Although the market as a whole has been flat since then, the Retton stock price closed yesterday at $58. The offer is share-for-share, with Motley stock worth $63 a share. That amounts to nine times Retton's earnings last year—which is, confidentially, roughly what we estimate they'll earn again *this* year.

Motley has had a history of expansion through acquisitions and its earnings have grown erratically. Its own stock has been selling at a premium to earnings in line with a lot of similar companies. It's not exactly Beatrice Foods, which made hundreds of acquisitions over the course of a couple of decades. (Why I am telling *you* this; didn't you write something about Beatrice when we were in school?) But you could say Motley's central business is mergers with good companies that have a much lower multiple of earnings. So far the strategy has worked well, though there haven't been any dramatic hits.

On the other hand, Retton may have too much of a commitment to the *status quo*. I don't mean they're 100 percent closed to new ideas, but they are generally reluctant to terminate a product or a division. They always find some reason for continuing to manufacture and distribute products that were once successful but aren't now, so long as the product has a band of loyal customers, however small.

Well, with that kind of situation, how should we answer Motley's tender offer? (Sorry, Daisy. That's not really a question for you. It's the question I'm asking *myself* these days.) The Retton Salaried Employees Retirement Trust holds 10 percent of Retton's outstanding stock. Also, something like 7 percent of the trusts we manage here hold Retton shares. Some of those shares were inherited and some were bought at our suggestion.

My specific assignment is to decide whether to accept Motley's offer on behalf of the trusts we manage. Obviously we could tip the balance of the war in favor of Motley if we were to tender our stock. I don't think anyone at Retton thinks there's a real risk of our doing *that*, but their lawyers said we're the ones who have to make the decision, so here I am. Some random thoughts:

1. A price of nine times earnings is not ridiculously high for the stock. Retton has sold at this level before.

2. Retton management has been able to maintain its dividend for the last five years and has the earnings to support it. This yield is better than the Dow 30-stock average.

3. Motley says it will liquidate certain unprofitable Retton operations when it gets control, and there's no reason to think it won't, given its past procedures to increase the earnings of acquired companies. One Retton operation that's been stumbling lately is the barbell plant not far from my house. We have a pretty stiff unemployment rate in town, and any additional lay-offs would make a lot of families unhappy. Not to mention add to the financial burden of a county that's already operating in the red, thanks to our local treasurer's aggressive trading in long-term Treasuries. (You may have heard about *that* one!)

4. We wouldn't want to own Motley stock for any length of time. Too risky. Looking back, you can see why Motley sold at a price earnings multiple higher than the market, but I sure wouldn't want to be the one to predict its future earnings or stock prices. So if we tendered and the tender were successful, we would want to sell the Motley stock promptly. On the other

hand, if we declined to tender and Motley won anyway, our accounts might end up in a minority position. Under these circumstances, our stock might not bring the $42 a share it was selling for last year: there's no reason to assume Motley would expand its tender offer once it achieved control.

5. Theoretically, if we were convinced Motley was going to lose, we could sell our Retton stock in the market now at $58 and then buy it back at, say, $40 after the smoke cleared. But that's a short-term operation and even if Motley *did* lose we'd have to be very skillful and very right. Can you see me at an X-shaped desk, playing Michael Milken? Hell, I'm not a speculator. There's a risk, too, that the trade would put a block in the hands of Motley, enabling them to win after all. The penalty for being wrong would be a big blow, not just in regard to Retton and the local community but with our other customers. I mean, we stand to lose our entire image of reliability here. Even if we sold and bought back the Retton shares and Motley lost, Retton wouldn't be happy with what would look like our walking out on their interests. And justifiably so.

Sorry to hit you with all this so suddenly, Daisy. Just need a sensible ear to bend every once in awhile. Any advice or comments welcome. My best to David and the boys. And where are those photographs you promised me?

Chan to MacReed:
Hi Ros. Good to hear from you even if it's in full paragraphs. I've just put the boys to bed so everything's quiet here, but give me a minute to get my thinking cap on!

The first thing I'll say is this: you seem to have identified the major issues confronting you as an analyst and portfolio manager. But are you sure your notes aren't simply preparation for a decision already made in line with Retton's expectations? In other words, that the 10 and 7 percent blocks represent a secure vote for management? I notice you're at least considering the idea of selling into the market in order to take advantage of the run-up in price. That's an imaginative, albeit unlikely, twist to the current controversy. But the overall impression I get is that you're systematically knocking down all the alternatives to the mainstream answer—namely, sticking with Retton management. If that's the game, I don't want to play. Are you being straight with me and with yourself?

You begin with your technical responsibility for investments, analyzing the reasonableness of the offered price, but your analysis is pretty shallow. (Hey, you always said you valued my honesty!) Then you shift to the impact of a takeover, identifying who could be adversely affected: the community, local Retton employees, and, by inference, your firm.

You touch on the adverse consequences to the fund's Retton holdings if the takeover is rejected, but you also recognize that this holding is not simply a piece of paper: it's an investment in a real entity, just as a theater "company" is more than the script, the house and the producer's money, but also includes individual actors, the director, all the backstage employees. And, for a given performance, the audience in the house. Who does that suggest should be on your list in the Retton case? Who comes first, and last?

It's never comfortable to question whether an analysis is made in good faith. Certainly it would be unrealistic for a person in your position (Senior Vice-President and going higher, now maybe responsible for deciding whether one of your company's major clients lives or dies) to ignore the probable outcome of the analysis, which will be to support Retton and continue with the investment. But if your analysis is simply documentation that was supplied to support a prefabricated conclusion, your notes aren't worth the paper they're written on (if they ever made it to paper.)

Yours in cyber-space,
Daisy

MacReed to Chan:
Ouch! But I appreciate your giving me a kick in the behind. It's easy to get carried away supporting the people you know. I like the people at Retton. I

think they're doing a good job, although their devotion to antiquity does make me crazy. And I want to see them continue. They've made a commitment to their employees that you just don't see much anymore. IBM. AT&T. Kodak. Every time you turn around, another blue chip company is laying off 10,000 people.

On the other hand, I have to live with change. One thing Professor Mayer managed to hammer into my head when we had him back in B-school is that if you spend tomorrow waiting for what happened yesterday, you're going to get burned. So I do try to anticipate what might occur regardless of whether I like it or not.

Maybe I outlined Motley's offer too quickly during our conversation. It's taking up so much of my time these days, I sometimes forget that other people have actual lives. Motley has its thumb in numerous pies. In the last four or five years they must have acquired half a dozen companies in different businesses, from eye drops to mortgages. Their tactic is generally to negotiate the acquisitions after taking an investment position and pushing the target management into a corner. That's exactly what happened here. Motley bought pretty steadily for a couple of months, then sat back. There was no blip in the stock price or obvious increase in the volume of trades. Retton was basically clueless.

Four months passed. Retton's reported earnings dropped. The company had no new products to announce, pricing was rigid, costs were steadily escalating. The price of the stock dipped a couple of points and finally one week Motley slurped up all the shares it could find. At 9 percent, Motley announced its tender offer. I understand they called Retton's CEO to say it was going to happen. I think it was a Friday when the call came. The offer was going to be made public the following Monday. I guess the tone was superficially friendly, but who's kidding who? In any event, the tender offer was then spelled out for 41 percent more of Retton stock at $63 per share. First come, first served. Nothing for those who don't tender.

$63 is a good price. When Retton sold at nine times earnings a number of years ago, sports stores were really just taking off. You could make a good case for an expansion in basic items like tennis rackets and running shoes. The trend now is toward wilderness sports. People want backpacks and kayaks. It's hard to keep up when you're based in big-city Ohio.

I admit there are stockholder advantages to selling off some of the unprofitable businesses and going with the high demand products. Even the barbell plant is marginal and not important to the rest of the business. Speaking locally, though, it doesn't have to be liquidated. It's an integrated operation that could be sold by Retton to its employees under certain reasonable financing agreements. Probably with increased employee incentives it could provide a living for its workers and not be a drain on Retton as far as future earnings growth is concerned. Sale of the plant would also provide added capital over time that could be used to develop some of Retton's retail stores.

But I certainly can't see that sort of employee stock ownership deal being worked out by Motley. They'd just close the plant down and auction off half the company in order to end up with a few small divisions that happen to adhere to some grand design. What a waste. It would have been just a fancy exercise in arithmetic. It would affect the pension beneficiaries in unknown ways, throw good people out of work, change expectations for local residents, and break up a team that makes products customers have confidence in. It doesn't make sense. It's not as though we bought the 10 percent of Retton stock to protect management. It's been in the fund for years.

Sorry, Daisy. Didn't mean to get shrill. And I realize I haven't done much in the way of numbers. I will. Tomorrow. Guess I'm going to have to get over this attachment to Retton, huh? Still attached to you, though. Best to the various menfolk.

Reaction:

_____

_____

_____

_____

_____

_____

_____

_____

_____

_____

_____

_____

_____

Stockholders, Stakeholders

The central conflict troubling MacReed is the one between her allegiance to her client, Retton, and her allegiance to the beneficiaries of her client's retirement fund. What makes the situation difficult is the possibility that, in looking out for Retton's interests, MacReed may well be acting pragmatically with reference to her employer. After all, Retton pays the bills. If Motley absorbs the company, the new Motley/Retton conglomerate might take its fund business elsewhere. But can you see how this practical accommodation infringes on the interests of the people whom Prescient, and Rosalyn MacReed, are bound to protect?

Beyond *this* conflict are several more. Beneficiaries, both of the Retton retirement fund and of the personal trusts managed by Prescient, stand to gain a good deal of money if MacReed votes Prescient's proxies in favor of the Motley Group tender offer. Prescient owes a fiduciary duty to these beneficiaries, which might seem to make MacReed's decision clear.

But at least with regard to Retton's retirees, present and future, the matter isn't so simple. If Retton ceases to exist, future retirees may lose their jobs. Present retirees are of course less threatened by this prospect, but even they stand to lose *something*. First, Retton is a major player in the local economy. If the company's operations cease or are downsized in the area, the economy as a whole will suffer. There will be fewer jobs. City services may have to be cut back. Crime might increase, and neighborhoods deteriorate. Is this something MacReed should think about when considering her duties to Retton's retirees? Or are these contingencies too remote?

And what about another interest of the retirees, both present and future? Do the people who have worked for Retton have some sort of psychic interest in seeing the company continue? "Psychic interest"? You won't find it in the glossary of your Economics textbook. In fact, it sounds vaguely loony. But what about pride in a workplace? What about loyalty to a company? If they exist, can they be figured into the sort of decision MacReed faces?

In some respects, MacReed is dealing with a dichotomy often brought up in a slightly different context in relation to corporate takeovers. In considering whether a takeover is good or bad, whose interests should a director of the company take into account? Just the shareholders? Or should he consider also the interests of people—employees, customers, neighbors—who are "stakeholders" in the company? Most analysts believe that maximizing shareholder value (in other words, *getting the best price*) is a director's only duty. Stakeholders don't matter. Do you agree?

One problem often brought up in discussing stakeholder interests is the difficulty in quantifying those interests. It's one thing to figure out if a board of directors has gotten a good price for the company's shares. How can we—and how can MacReed—calculate the impact of the proposed takeover on Retton's home community? Here the offer is to exchange volatile Motley stock for Retton shares. That might be a killer for the pension fund. But what if the offer were cash? It seems fair to say that if concerns of the community are to override the demonstrable benefit to pensioners of tendering their shares at $63, these concerns ought to be pretty significant. How many jobs would be lost? How mobile are the people who would be laid off? Are there alternative sources of work, so that the period of unemployment for those who do lose their jobs would be short? How likely are these assumptions?

More on the people question. Are retraining options available to help ameliorate the negative effects of the anticipated lay-offs? Is the barbell plant the only one at risk, and is a spin-off to the employees a realistic possibility? Is it possible that Retton, responding to its own need to remain viable, would also be likely to close down some or all of the plants in question? Is it an open-and-shut case that the shareholders would in the long run lose all opportunity for appreciation staying with Retton, or is there a possibility that $63 a share would be realized over a period of time whether or not Motley is successful? If the company is worth $63 to Motley, is there $63 of value if Retton pulls up its socks? If MacReed's decision is to hold the shares in perpetuity, will the probable flow of dividends and growth of capital compare favorably over time with other alternatives? The questions keep coming.

None of this is to say that Rosalyn MacReed is necessarily acting irresponsibly in trying to promote the welfare of Retton's home community. It's just that, given a) Prescient's close relationship with Retton management on the one hand and b) the obvious advantages that will accrue to Retton's fund beneficiaries if the Motley Group tender offer is accepted, MacReed is going to have to work harder to justify her decision on the basis of stakeholder interests.

Deciding in Light of Future Decisions

How MacReed acts here can establish an example for her successors in similar situations. It's not just a matter of outcome. Even a good decision reached inarticulately sets a bad precedent for the future, since there is no record of the process used to reach the decision.

MacReed could explore selling the pension fund holding to Retton at, say, $58 a share, the current market price, or perhaps work out a put option at a lesser figure, preserving the opportunity that might result from the merger threat. Should she go beyond her gut reaction that the longtime holding of the 10 percent Retton position is to be continued and seek outside advice from the participants in the plan as to their desires? Or from a professional consultant? In pursuing even those participatory devices, she should recognize that either or both can be misused, manipulated to ratify a desired decision, and cause stress and loss of control instead of increasing openness and decentralizing the process.

New situations can be envisioned to test the decision as a precedent. For example, how would MacReed handle the Retton stock if Motley were also one of Prescient's major customers? What if *Retton* were to announce plans to close down its unprofitable plants, including the local barbell factory, and Motley countered by announcing that it intended to keep them open?

Such questions get at whether the negative effect on a local community is real or merely an advocate's argument. It's only human for MacReed to conclude that her neighbor is the good guy and the out-of-towner an adversary. All the more reason to utilize a systematic approach when analyzing the situation—first considering the best interests of those who rely on her, in this case the pension beneficiaries, and then raising suspicions about any conclusion that conveniently supports her own career.

Chapter 11

The Sop of Soft Dollars: Figuring Out Who Pays (1988)

The back-scratching arrangements our hero has finally grown tired of are depressingly familiar in the financial world. What complicates matters here is that he himself has profited from these arrangements.

We've seen how acting ethically in the financial industry requires not only good intentions but also a great deal of knowledge about how specific transactions work. Without a grasp of such details, the alternatives to a given action cannot be identified, let alone measured properly against each other—especially since the details of a deal or operation may be constantly changing, especially at the margins. But figuring out who will be effected by a transaction, and how those effects will be felt, requires more than mere facts. It requires imagination.

The Possibility of Redemption

Because institutional investors execute a myriad of transactions in stocks, bonds, and other securities, the captain of an institution's trading desk is constantly making decisions that affect investment results for its customers. One such decision is this: which brokerage firm will be chosen to execute a given trade? Sounds easy. Pick the broker with the lowest commission. Right? But there may be good reasons for a fiduciary not to select a given broker for a particular transaction. For example, its execution might be less effective. Its finances might be shaky. It might be unable to handle large blocks of securities, or incapable of providing desirable insights into the market.

There may also be less legitimate reasons for going to the higher-priced broker—reasons like friendship, social connections, or the provision of services that the institution is itself paid to perform. Often such services are paid for in "soft dollars," which isn't currency at all but rather services or perquisites that don't show up on the books. Market research is one such soft dollar benefit. But brokers have been known to reward the loyalty of institutional investors with less defensible soft dollar benefits as well, as the following case shows.

The scene is laid at Mas Fina Cantina, hard by the offices of Chicago's Bigelow Trust Company, a trustee for many regional pension accounts. Standing at the bar is Bigelow Trust Company's head trader, Leo Wittenberg, a beetle-browed Fotomat of a man in his mid 40s.

"You hear me okay?" he shouts. Though the NBA play-offs are blaring from above the bourbon bottles, we hear him just fine.

Okay, so I got a problem. You want to hear about it? You buy me another Bud and I'll tell you more than you want to know. I've been working at Bigelow's trading desk for more years than I care to admit. Before that, when I was just a kid, I worked for a couple of the retail brokers. *Wirehouses*, they call 'em. So I've been around.

In the old days, when commissions were fixed, we at Bigelow pretty much divided up our business among the brokers with local offices. In 1975 the game changed. Transaction commissions were deregulated, see? The major firms in the business developed similar discounted fee schedules but continued to provide us with research by the pound and we stuck with them.

We're always under pressure from our pension fund customers for good investment ideas, and we handle the bond market okay but need all the stock research we can get. If we dealt with some no-name pipe rack firm in New York, we'd get zero research in return. Zilch. Besides which, discounters like that don't position securities, so large block trades are out of the question with them. They're fine for self-help investors, but hey, who even *knows* these guys? You know?

The old-line firms around town are just the opposite: they understand that we're accountable and that trading expenses could kill the golden goose if our performance suffers. Their commissions all fall within the same range. They throw us all sorts of investment ideas, and they throw us a few shares of new stock issues that are rationed out because of high demand. There's nothing as tantalizing as knowing that a new stock is going to sell above the offering price because the issue is already presold and the unsatisfied demand will push up the after-market. Their stocks—high-tech, high-risk type ventures—don't fit in with our pension customers' portfolios. But it's great for the morale of the fellas at Bigelow to be allocated those stocks for their own accounts. Hell, I know it's great for *my* morale. And there's no real problem with it. No competition for the shares with our customers. I pick the brokers, but not the stock our clients are going to invest in. And I don't have the authority to churn anyone's account, since buy and sell orders come from another department.

We get more than just service from the brokers. We also get a lot of business from them. Brokers make loans to their customers. It's an important revenue source for the brokers and, when we lend that money to the broker, important to us, too. With long-distance discounters, you don't see any of that. I don't mean we only pick the brokers who have loans with us. We go to the block traders—the big boys like Salomon Brothers and Goldman Sachs—whenever we have to move a lot of shares in a hurry. But the trust officers don't march in lock-step and most of our activity is buying and selling for the different accounts spread over a period of time—100 share lots, without a need to do much in the way of block transactions. We're long-term investors for our customers.

One of our major sources of information is Jerry Grottle over at Escutcheon Brokerage Services. Escutcheon deals in small company stocks in the over-the-counter market.

Jerry does a lot of local research. Of course we trade mostly in the big national stocks but we've also established a niche with a few of the more established local companies, representing them and salting customer portfolios with their stock. Escutcheon makes a market in most of the local stocks we deal with, so it's like calling directly to a specialist on the floor of the exchange.

You have to get to know people to have a sense of their reliability. That's important in making judgment calls. We know Jerry and his firm pretty well and see them after hours. They have these box seats for the Bulls games that we have access to, pretty much whenever we want. We've been strict about it, though: we have a rule that we rotate the seats among the execs here and you're always supposed to take a customer or prospect, not just your wife or kid or somebody. Every year there's a chance to go to the Super Bowl for Escutcheon's best customers and you can be sure Bigelow is at the top of that list. Usually Wally Stein, our president, goes, and takes a couple of the bank's independent directors. We always joke that one of these days he's going to bring back a bunch of shirts that say, MY C.E.O. WENT TO THE SUPER BOWL AND ALL I GOT WAS THIS LOUSY T-SHIRT.

Officers get a commission on any new business we bring to the bank. In my position, I've been able to introduce a lot of new customers Grottle has sent me. Seems like every doctor has a broker these days and you find they have pension plans where they need a bank to act as custodian and manager and to keep the records. There's loan business for the commercial side of the bank, as I mentioned, and some tax shelter opportunities at the end of the year.

Well, as you work with the brokers and they become confident you're not going to take their customers away, they're happy to throw you more business. It's the old story, I guess: The more you work together, the more you *can* work together.

I mentioned hot issues. Well, Jerry's my personal broker and he's been a lot of help. A slew of new companies in this part of the country come to market in the O.T.C., and I've built up a nice little portfolio over the years. Sometimes, if the demand is really wild, I sell out, but usually I buy and hold. Over a period of time, several of these little companies have had mergers and ended up listed on one of the exchanges. Then again every once in a while one of them tanks, so you have to put together a pretty good assortment in order to make it work. Anyway, Jerry keeps me in mind and gives me a call whenever he sees something interesting coming along. And like I said: There's no conflict with the pension funds because they don't buy high risk.

Besides that, we have a compliance department that keeps us on our toes. There's a "Chinese wall" between the loan department and the traders, so we don't even know about new deals the bank is financing until they're up and running. Once, just by chance, I sold some stock I owned just before the announcement of a big loan to finance an acquisition and the price took a tumble. Well, Bigelow's compliance guy was all over me. *How did you know about the acquisition?* he says. I didn't, I say. *Can you prove it?* he says. Prove what? *That you didn't know.* Of course I can't prove I didn't know. What are you, Hans Kafka? *So why did you sell your shares?* I had a hunch, okay? Finally he pulled in his claws. But it just goes to show, they really watch those things.

Sounds great, huh? I ain't got a problem in the world. Except for my stupid head. See, sometimes I think too much. Maybe it's age, and getting close to retirement. Maybe it's thinking about Wally's clique in the bank and getting a couple of lemons from Jerry Grottle. And my kid, the lawyer, pushing me about how it's my customers' buying power, not mine, that gets old Jerry Grottle's interest. About how it's the customers' money that's buying me my start-up stocks, and Wally Stein his trips to Super Sunday. And how they may set me up as a scapegoat, Jerry and Wally, if the SEC ever comes sniffing around.

I ain't saying I'm Mother Teresa. No way. But lately I keep thinking about something my father told me. He always said, never do anything you wouldn't want your grandfather to know about. Everyone's got some saying like that. You know. Don't do anything you wouldn't want to see on the front page of the *New York Times*. Don't do anything you wouldn't want to see on the 6 o'clock news. With him it was his grandfather. Which was fine. I mean, his grandfather came over from Lithuania. Saved his pennies. Wore the same pair of pants for nine years. But *my* grandfather, I never knew him. Which is maybe why I never took the saying seriously. Now I find out my kid's wife is going to have a baby. A little boy. So maybe what I want is to be clean for the kid. You know. Give him something to look up to.

Fact is, Bigelow is losing trust business because we haven't been in the big winners. Jerry isn't in that league and I've been the patsy who stuck up for him. Anyway I felt I'd better protect myself. So about a week ago I wrote up a little confidential memo. Sent it to Stein and a couple of the other brass icons. It said:

> The other night after work I had a beer with some investment types as I occasionally do. They were complaining about the other banks in town tightening up on commissions and trades. Jerry Grottle was fit to be tied, as you can imagine. There's some software a lot of the banks are getting that collates the cents per share on each transaction into a report and ignores the way we've always done

it—just showing total dollars, or sometimes the discount from the 1975 Stock Exchange Commission Schedule, like "40 percent off." Of course, our paperwork doesn't show anything except the price on new issues or trades in the over-the-counter market. That's always been fine for us and our customers have never asked for anything else as far as I know. (Though who knows *what* they'll be wanting in the future, with all the plaintiff's bar litigation going on these days!)

One of Grottle's guys mentioned a lawsuit filed against some big trust company in New York for choosing brokers who are their own loan customers. And a fund manager said the SEC was making noises about brokers getting commission business from mutual funds they bring customers to. I'm no lawyer and I don't know what it was all about, but everyone was talking doomsday. Old Matty Costanza got so excited he almost choked on a pretzel, at which point Joey the bartender came around to give him the Hemlock Maneuver but Matty spat the pretzel up on his own and says you touch me, ginslinger, and you get the Hemlock Maneuver where not even your doctor's gonna find it. We were rollin' in the aisles.

But to get back to the point, another fellow even said he'd gone to some compliance conference and heard about these firms that make you clear all your personal trades before you make them. We've been pretty liberal on all that and as far as I can see it's never hurt our customers. We have a lot of very good people working at Bigelow and if they take a step you can be pretty sure it's all right. But with all of the talk I got a little upset about whether there might be criticism of the bank and whether you want me to do something about guidelines. Maybe write something up. Any advice or suggestions would be welcome.

P.S. I've sent a copy of this memo to Aaron Wechsel over in legal, just in case he has some ideas on all this.

Well, I disguised it as well as I could, but I'm pretty sure Stein and those guys will be able to see through the Groucho glasses. *Leo Wittenberg? Wants to write guidelines?* And it's not that I haven't done all right by myself as well. But at some point you gotta take a stand. Either stand up or let the money train roll over you, right?

Problem is, somebody here leaked the memo to Grottle over at Escutcheon, who called me this afternoon. He's not about to start spitting on my grave—hell, nobody knows if I'm going to be a goat or a hero at Bigelow at this point—but he sure let me know not to count on any favors for awhile. Let me know he didn't appreciate the way I paid him back for the shares he'd thrown my way in the past as well. Made me feel pretty damned bad, as a matter

of fact. So much for loyalty, huh? I guess that's
why they call me the head traitor.

So maybe I did the wrong thing. But like I say,
sometimes you gotta take a stand. Let's hope this
one doesn't turn out like Custer's.

Reaction:

_____

_____

_____

_____

_____

_____

_____

_____

_____

_____

_____

_____

_____

_____

Getting Sucked In

The back-scratching arrangements our hero has finally
grown tired of are depressingly familiar in the financial
world. What complicates matters here is that he himself
has profited from these arrangements. What do you think
of his attempt to extricate himself from the web?

Start from the point of view of pragmatism. All things considered, has Leo Wittenberg acted in the best interests of his employer? Is he now? Though management at Bigelow seems comfortable (extremely comfortable) with the system of kickbacks and entertainment perks flowing from Escutcheon, is this system really helping Bigelow, its customers and shareholders? For whatever reasons, even in the near-term, things now seem to be coming unstuck. Leo Wittenberg may in fact be the first person at Bigelow even to question the *status quo*. But what about the litigation Wittenberg has heard rumors of?

Despite his past enjoyment of Jerry Grottle's "extras," isn't Wittenberg's action praiseworthy from the perspectives of justice and rights? Does his questionable motive undo the good of the action? He does seem genuinely concerned about the costs to Bigelow's customers involved in the entertainment extras supplied by Escutcheon—costs so well hidden that those customers have yet to complain about them.

So perhaps Wittenberg is acting ethically here. If a decision is ethical only if it works, his elliptical tack may be the wisest one to take. Let's hope the big man makes a difference at Bigelow as we move on to a closer consideration of the issues he's brought up in his monologue.

Hard Questions on Soft Dollars

The distinction between benefits to the bank and benefits to the bank's customers is sometimes a difficult one to draw. Who pays? Who receives the benefits? Ideally, the questions have a common answer.

It's hard to believe a brokerage firm like Escutcheon is charging the lowest price for services (the negotiated commission if it is acting as a broker/agent; the spread between bid and asked prices if it's acting as principal/dealer). After all, *someone* has to pay for the entertainment and other perks Jerry Grottle dispenses to the purchasing agents at his institutional clients. Transactions in the over-the-counter market, where price and commission are bundled together, can be particularly vulnerable to this type of exploitation.

The Bigelow pattern involves a series of potential problems. Higher turnover generates more commissions. Congenial negotiations on commissions allow more profits for the broker, resulting in fewer commissions for other brokers and less research *from* them. Meanwhile, Jerry Grottle has his entertainment budget.

Professional trustees are likely to have discretion over the selection of the broker executing transactions as part of their job of managing portfolios. This is also true of an in-house pension committee running a retirement benefit fund and of institutional intermediaries such as investment managers and insurance companies. In the bond market, choosing a broker is essential to the effectiveness of a transaction: the specific security selected will depend on availability and price at the moment. By way of contrast, transactions in listed stocks can often be placed with any of several brokers who offer good competitive executions. This reflects not only the high level of competence of many brokerage firms, but also the massive volume and high-quality mechanics of the exchange markets.

The Research Rationale

Wittenberg has shown that there are real conflicts of interest between the broker/dealer and the investor, and between the investor and the investor's representative who selects the broker. Hockey tickets, a credit line on someone else's American Express Card, new business possibilities, and personal investment opportunities are temptations that can smack of fraud on the customer.

Investment research is different, as it can be a fringe benefit that really aids the customer. From an ethical point of view, since research is closely tied to client results, it is a proper item to take into account in the selection between otherwise competitive brokers. For instance, suppose that an institution called Mefford Bank & Trust wants to buy a hundred shares of General Motors stock, and that GM is the kind of stock sold by most brokers with equal effectiveness. Brokers X, Y, and Z will execute the transaction at the same price, 10 cents a share. A code of ethics recently formulated by Mefford prohibits acceptance of gifts and favors (including new business introductions) with a value over $25 as criteria for the selection of brokers for client transactions. In the past, investment research offered by Broker Z has been useful to the customers. Under the circumstances, Z is selected.

Even with a rule like this, there can be conflicts. What if Broker Z had signed a contract to provide on-line research to Mefford for a year in return for a specific "soft dollar" figure of commissions from customer accounts? There are two potential distortions in the process of selection: pressure on customers' accounts to generate the specific dollar amount of brokerage apart from investment needs, and pressure to choose Broker Z for any particular transaction. If last year's commissions for bank customers totaled a million dollars and the firm made a million-dollar commitment to brokers for research for this year, the pressures would be enormous and obvious. If the commitments only totaled $10,000, the pressure would be minimal. Rough justice is not necessarily unethical. In an ideal world, this question will be asked each time: "Is this transaction occurring to generate the agreed-on dollars or is it for genuine investment needs?"

A practical, publicized and enforced code of ethics is essential—as is the intelligence and experience of a man like Leo Wittenberg, who sees the ethical problems facing his firm and has set out, however haltingly, to bring his employer around to facing them. True, he himself has benefited from Jerry Grottle's soft dollars. Maybe he's not acting in spite of this fact, but *because* of it. Maybe Wittenberg has, in fact, had the imagination to recognize that the one inevitable casualty of the unethical decision is the person who makes it.

Consider the Alternatives

There are as many paths as there are stars.

Lao Tse

Chapter 12

Leading and Misleading:
Outing the Options (1994)

An individual investor can think whatever he wants to about a stock. An outside director has an obligation to think harder.

Corporate directors can get confused as to which of several constituencies they represent when they make decisions. It's easy, for example, for outside directors to fall into the trap of thinking the corporation they work for is the group of senior officers they see at board meetings. This misperception can lead in turn to unwise and shortsighted results. When does a good decision become a bad one? Is it ever easy to admit you were wrong? Is it ever necessary?

Alliances

DOS/X Corporation is a publicly-held company engaged in the production and distribution of tax accounting software for use by the comptrollers of state and municipal governments. As DOS/X has recently sustained significant losses, a special meeting of the board was called to discuss the viability of the firm and a possible merger with Superior Systems, Inc. (SSI), an up-and-coming competitor created by two programmers who'd defected from DOS/X only three years before. The logic of the proposed merger was obvious. DOS/X had service and distribution strengths supporting a moribund product line, while SSI was creating state-of-the-art specialty software but having trouble getting its client agencies online and accustomed to the new systems.

Our protagonist is George Grinnell, an experienced management and securities analyst who is an outside director of DOS/X and a member of the board's audit committee. Excerpts from his recent letter to the author follow.

> All of us directors were nervous about the erosion of the company's capital base. The stock was holding on at 9 1/2 but would drop fast when the bad news came out about our latest losses. Charlie Carlton, who's been President of DOS/X since he created the company in his kitchen 23 years ago, had kept in touch with the guys who organized SSI and he reported that there was a chance of doing a deal with SSI to keep DOS/X alive.

> SSI is a private company and not interested in having public shareholders. That could have been worked out. We could have preserved our listing on NASDAQ while giving SSI control on some basis. They just wanted our service network, really. The deal they offered provided that four officers of DOS/X, including Charlie Carlton, would receive two-year employment contracts with SSI at their current

salary levels and that DOS/X shareholders would receive $10 a share, making DOS/X a wholly-owned subsidiary of SSI. I did some research and gave a formal opinion that $10 was a fair price—maybe not the best price, but fair overall—for the DOS/X shares, and we announced the merger plan for the shareholders to approve.

Just before the shareholders' meeting, though, Reliance Software made a cash tender offer for all the shares of DOS/X at $12.50. The offer was contingent on the rejection of the proposed merger between DOS/X and SSI. And it was a shock, I'll tell you. But you could see the logic here, too. Reliance saw SSI as a real threat, especially if they were to combine with us. And Reliance, too, though it was considerably older, had marketing and distribution problems. So in buying DOS/X, Reliance would be killing two birds with one stone: strengthening itself while shutting out a competitor. Only problem was, Charlie and his gang figured they'd be out on their butts if Reliance took over the company. We adjourned the shareholders' meeting for a couple of weeks and then again for a month in order to discuss all this with SSI. In early August, Charlie came back to the board with the first smile he'd managed in weeks and a new deal he'd been able to work out under which SSI would pay *$14* a share for the DOS/X common.

Well, Charlie said we had to act fast. In retrospect, I suppose I should have at least asked him if he'd ever actually sat down with the folks at Reliance to ask them about their plans for the company. After all, they hadn't exactly *said* they were going to dump anyone. We were all just assuming.

But by now everyone was charged up about the new plan. I tried to say something to a couple of the other directors, but it was like I was Long John Silver or something. *Threatening mutiny! Plotting to kill Cap'n Charlie!* You've got to understand the respect we all had for Charlie. There isn't a better guy in the business. Bright. Creative. The kind of guy who can make his employees feel like they're coming home when they show up at work. So I kept my mouth shut.

To nail down the deal, we agreed to give SSI a one-year irrevocable option to buy enough unissued shares at $14 a share to equal 200 percent of our current capital. That meant they would be sure to have the two-thirds vote needed to approve the merger, no matter what stock went to Reliance. We drafted up a letter to the shareholders announcing the new agreement and advised them not to tender to Reliance.

By that point it was getting hard to focus on anything else but the merger machinations. As you can guess, we spent a lot of time going back and forth on the telephone, and there were some stories in the press and a lot of inquiries from brokers and shareholders. The transaction volume in the stock had really picked up as the speculators got in on the action, placing their casino bets. At that point, Reliance increased its offer to $15.50 a share on the condition that the DOS/X SSI option deal be terminated.

Well, you know the rest. I went with Charlie's plan. One day, when we get through with these damned lawsuits, and our shareholders realize the value of keeping Charlie Carlton around, I think they'll thank me for it.

Reaction:

_____

_____

_____

_____

_____

_____

_____

_____

_____

_____

_____

_____

_____

Silicon Samurai

Consider the importance of practicality in a financial decision. Factor in fairness. Look at the rights of those affected. Then look at how George Grinnell conducted himself in connection with the DOS/X merger negotiations. Should George Grinnell have carried out the mutiny his fellow board members warned him against? That is to say, should he have insisted that, at a minimum, someone sit down with Reliance and ascertain the company's plan for DOS/X? Or was he right to charge ahead with the rest of the crew in support of Charlie Carlton's flag?

The process by which DOS/X management sold out, or tried to, was inadequate by any standard. The shareholders had a right to participate in the decision, but communication to (and from) the shareholders was severely short-circuited here. If the DOS/X board members had any belief that they were acting properly, it was because they were transfixed by short-term horizons and something that smells like team spirit. Their team included the senior officers and probably the company's creditors. Conceivably, DOS/X's finances were so meager that its creditors in effect already "owned" the outfit and were being treated as though they were the preferred shareholders.

The members of the team who were left behind included the true shareholders. They were treated as though they were unable to make a decision that would affect them. No distinction was made between those shareholders whose financial incompetence required reliance on outside experts such as the DOS/X board, and others who could have fended for themselves if they had had the information to which they were entitled.

Is this a question of 20/20 hindsight? Would there have been any ethical problem if Reliance had not made its offer? Maybe not. But it seems clear that the process itself lacked equity. The decision was to take the company private and cut off any future opportunity for the shareholders whom the board was supposedly representing and to do so without testing the best price. Grinnell's *pro forma* $10 appraisal was a key element.

Maybe the problem arose because Grinnell began and ended with price. A better starting point might have been the "social contract" that management is to run the company under the informed guidance of the board for the benefit of all the shareholders. This benchmark would have had very practical applications when Grinnell, as a putative independent, came to the question of whether he could give an objective opinion on the fairness of SSI's offer.

Not to be hard on Grinnell. At the first stage of the merger, the stock price may have seemed fair. The deal benefited the shareholders by a slightly better than market price. It also benefited the corporate management team that Grinnell had been working with and, not coincidentally, Charlie Carlton himself, who presumably had a hand in appointing Grinnell to the board. It's true that management promoted its self-interest by developing employment contracts with SSI, but this was disclosed to the shareholders, and Grinnell may very well have acted in good faith, seeing this as a legitimate deal.

The ethical difficulty arose in the next stage, when the facts changed dramatically. Despite the Board's tunnel vision, an alternative to Charlie Carlton's plan dropped into their laps. And when Reliance added a 25 percent premium to the price, Grinnell and the board ought to have rethought the situation. The actions of the new contender had proved Grinnell's assumption wrong. This was not just a friendly and routine deal. At this point he should have started over again—admittedly, a difficult task for anyone.

But instead of reevaluating the situation when the facts changed, Grinnell marched forward with the pack to find a way to complete the original deal before Wall Street took over. As a professional, he should have discarded his earlier appraisal and prepared a new one. By producing another analysis, he could have investigated alternatives, demanding more details of the Reliance offer and its effect on the company. Instead he allowed himself to be used as a shield for the SSI option arrangement, so that no matter what the shareholders decided, a price of $14 would be impregnable.

Since—excepting only the paltry qualms expressed by Grinnell himself—there is no indication of any disunity among the members of the board, it would appear the decision was taken unanimously. Not only was Reliance being blocked, but so was any other bidder who might have paid a higher price. How is that fair?

Loyalty

Loyalty is a wonderful ethical underpinning of society. In the DOS/X-Reliance case, Grinnell was loyal to the team composed of Charlie Carlton and Grinnell's own colleagues on the board. In turn, after Carlton's difficult financial problem was solved by the commitment of SSI, SSI became another partner in this enterprise and another party to whom he gave his allegiance.

The problem is, loyalty to your buddies can be a trap. It can be the source of discrimination in employment, distortion in long-term planning, and failure to bring into a management group specialists—so-called "knowledge workers"—with a command of details and their implications for the financial health of an organization or transaction. Grinnell's need to extend his loyalty to the broader group of shareholders—to consider whether the deal was fair to them, or respected their rights—was forgotten. Whether his loyalty should have gone beyond even the shareholders to include suppliers, customers, and the local community wasn't addressed at all. Should it have been?

A Second Chance

Modern theater sometimes allows its audience to choose the ending it wants to see. If the events of the DOS/X situation were repeated in a situation in which you were involved, how would you act in light of the experience you have gained from Grinnell? How would you handle your role as director? When would you begin to act differently from Grinnell?

An analyst is added to a board because his or her skills and experience bring value and legitimacy to a company's management group. The fact that the board expresses a need for your particular services is apt to be part of the reason why you joined in the first place. You can provide new perspectives, and urge alternatives to the course of business as usual.

But what if, once on the board, you tend to be pleasant, bending your views to meet those of the other members who have a broader knowledge of the company, its history, and its goals? Deference is one thing, but there's an obvious catch-22 in this situation. You are valuable to the board because of your skills and knowledge, yet you reduce your value when you dilute and suppress your perceptions to conform with others. When you keep your mouth shut. When you go along.

If and when it becomes clear that a company with which you are affiliated may not survive on its own, you may have an opportunity, indeed a *responsibility*, to take command of the manner in which the issue at hand is analyzed. As a financial professional, you have been trained as a "numbers person," and can quantify the issues. Make a list of the issues and people affected by the company's troubles in some kind of order: creditors, customers, long-term suppliers, employees, officers, shareholders. Then begin to draft a methodology for the board, a structure for analyzing developments, deciding on an outline of who is to participate and what goals are to be achieved. You may be overruled and your best ideas may at times seem unimaginative and disappointing. Still, your efforts may ensure that the sole rallying point in the decision-making process will not be a distorted "rah-rah" definition of loyalty to those you see most often.

Most importantly, never be afraid to revise in the face of new alternatives. As the French say, *Il n'y a que les imbeciles qui ne changent pas d'avis.* (Only a fool never changes his mind.)

Make the Decision

If you have built castles in the clouds, very well.
Now build foundations under them.

Henry David Thoreau

Chapter 13

Woman of the Year:
Action and Inaction in Difficult
Circumstances (1992)

*It doesn't count to say that failing to decide is itself
a sort of decision. What is needed here is the right
kind of decision.*

The hardest part of making a well-informed decision may
be just that: *making the decision.* Sticking your neck
out. Committing yourself to a course of action that may,
despite your best efforts, be the wrong one. There are no
guarantees when it comes to human behavior. There are, in
fact, only calculated risks.

34-year-old C.E.O. Claire Monte has been on a winning
streak for years. Now that winning streak is at an end.
What follows are excerpts from various sources, the first of
which is a journal containing notes for Ms. Monte's
autobiography, *Lonely at the Top.*

I've been very fortunate in my career here.

I started in the mail room of Adman Inc. 13 years ago as a recently-graduated English literature major. Didn't have a clue about the advertising business. Didn't have a clue about *any* business, really. I was just working at the agency till my first novel vaulted to the top of the bestseller list, at which point I was going to toss my date stamper in the trash can and parachute down to Madison Avenue, where a limo would be waiting at the curb. With Barbara Walters clutching one bumper, desperate for an exclusive.

I think the only thing that saved me from getting fired those first few weeks was that I cared about details. I lacked a lot in motivation, but the first time I made a real mistake—sending to the wrong person a press release with a very personal note from one of our division directors—it really got my attention. I was just embarrassed, I guess. Like, I was too good for this job in the first place, and then I go and just about get myself fired from it. So I buckled down. And I averted several other disasters—*other people's* disasters—from that point on by personally checking every piece of mail I assembled. I appointed myself to be a sort of last-ditch quality-control director, and I caught everything from simple spelling errors to fouled-up enclosures and missing documents.

Eventually I was appointed to head the mail room. It still wasn't exactly a title to inspire awe in my fellow NYU grads, but Aubrey Maturin, the

President of Adman in those days, took an interest in me. He made sure I started getting things to do.

It was Aubrey who suggested to me the importance of filing systems and easy retrievability, which few of us paid much attention to in those days. I mean, everything was manual then. But as we started to automate, going to computers, I became more and more involved. I went from head of the mail room to head of the file department, which eventually became the "data services department." And Aubrey was also always the one to suggest, "Hey, let's get Monte's perspective on this one"—sometimes on a project where I had no skills and didn't even understand what the questions were. I can't count the nights I stayed at the office till midnight, frantically studying memos and proposals, making notes to myself, trying to plug myself in. Eventually I started meeting with clients as part of the Adman marketing team. I was there basically to show off our computers. Give folks a look at our imaging capability, show 'em our charts and projections. It sounds shameless but it worked. People just can't get enough of computers.

I was gratified but quite frankly terrified too when I was invited to help create Consolidated Media Enterprises, Adman's holding company, and asked to carry on as a "required voice" in our campaign to acquire several regional advertising and media companies. I wasn't much of a technician, but I did add some much-needed perspective in the development of CME's computer systems and what we needed in terms of software to consolidate our newly-acquired operations. My view was that we had to keep our costs down if we were going to make the mergers work. It wasn't exactly a novel point, but I became known for stressing it, and my nuts-and-bolts experience helped me pinpoint areas where we *could* cut costs.

I was named President of CME three years ago and Woman of the Year by the National Council of Woman Executives the year after that. For one evening, at least, I had my limousine. My only disappointment? Barbara Walters was nowhere to be seen.

In the years since then, CME has seen steady growth in earnings, in the last several quarters at 12-15%, reinvested for future growth. As retained earnings have grown, our share prices have risen as well— which has made good mergers easy to negotiate in turn. Now we're nearing completion of talks with Wright Brothers, a Chicago agency specializing in health food and young women's fashion. I hope to announce a merger within the next 90 days. This one will put us in the big leagues, with CME's stock moving from the American to the New York Stock Exchange. It's what we've all been working toward for so long. If Aubrey were still alive, I know he'd be proud.

FAX from Asher Rippon to Mary Kate Nakamura,
Wall Street Journal
April 9
Dear Mary Kate,
I'd be happy to talk to you in connection with your article about the exacting science and delicate art of investor relations. I have to say I'm a fan of your work. I really enjoyed your piece on Ivan Boesky's new Ethics Institute!
At any rate, just telephone my office to arrange a time or times for an interview. I look forward to meeting you.
Yours sincerely,

Asher Rippon
Vice President, Investor Relations

Confidential Log, Claire Monte
April 17
Just received a disturbing phone call from Herb Ailing, Chairman of Maxico. Maxico! Still our most rabid competitor. He says they've just learned that we've been using some of their copyrighted software without permission. Implied that we may all end up in court, though naturally that's the last thing he wants. Herb says he called just to alert me that some very big bucks are involved, as Maxico considers the system to be proprietary. Says we stole their software and have profited tremendously in the merger game from the unique ability of this particular program to integrate ad agency systems

and generate consolidated results. Oh, yeah. And his daughter's getting married. June 11. Could I possibly come?

As far as I know, this is a baseless claim. Maxico is out to torpedo us because they can't compete. They'll do anything to snag Wright Brothers, especially now that we're on the brink of a deal. But reporters can't distinguish between fact and fantasy, so I can't let this get around till I know what the hell is going on. If anything *is* going on. Let this out of the bag and Peter Jennings will be happy to find us guilty on the network news. Just hope Maxico is still trying to get its facts straight as well; that'll give us a little time. I told Herb he'd better be pretty damned sure of himself before he files, or we're going to have his head. And hey, congratulations on that wedding!

My main thought is that I can't let them do this to CME's shareholders. A claim like this could cut our stock price in half and blow confidence in our financials for years. The markets hate uncertainty almost as much as reporters like to stir it up.

What to do. For starters, I need to know how serious this claim is. Got to get more information. Is Maxico's infringement claim believable? Calm down, Claire. Use your logic. And common sense! How do *they* know what we're doing, anyway? Who's the source? One of those crazy hackers down in Internal Systems? Maybe our Human Resources department can do a security check on our computer people. God. A corporate mole. Making xeroxes

for Maxico after hours. Using our copy machines.
Drinking our coffee. Eating our Zagnuts.

Get it together, Claire.

Worst case. The news comes out. Maxico asks for
the moon and we don't have the insurance to cover
it. The street traders start to shoot craps with our
stock, selling short for themselves and their
customers, playing the rumors like banjo strings.
The Wright Brothers wipe the kielbasa juice off their
chins long enough to read the *Journal* and decide
maybe they're not so crazy about us after all. And
we float there like the *Lusitania*, waiting for U-boats.
So much for mergers. Why? 1) If we're to make
our budget and pay for the deal, we have to have the
savings our software gives us. A new system just
isn't going to be ready in time. 2) Our stock multiple
is based on a big trust factor. It's CME. I'm Claire
Monte. We make money, dammit. We've always
made money. Earnings have to keep on going up to
maintain the multiple, and without the multiple and
an upcurve in profits we won't be able to sign the
Wright Brothers despite the handshake.

Okay, Claire. Think. Think hard. Before you get
blown away.

Asher Rippon
April 18
That thing on? You sure? Okay. Now remember,
Ms. Nakamura. I get a copy of this tape, and, as
you've agreed, I can knock anything I say off the

record. Right? Okay. As Director of Investor Relations, a big part of my job is to think about the effect of the company's public statements on CME stock. The timing, the context. The *spin*, as they say in politics. Claire—Ms. Monte—has to keep all this in mind too, but she has so many other things to worry about that she relies a lot on what I come up with. And even though I say "spin," I like to think we're a bit less obsessed with our image than the politicians are. I mean, look at me. I couldn't live with myself if I thought I was like, I don't know, a *PR* guy—even though that's exactly what I'm supposed to be. I just try to tell the truth. Since CME has been so successful over the past few years, it's been easy.

My background is in finance. That was my major in business school, and—excuse me? Oh. Oregon State. Go, Beavers! All the dates are on the resume you got. But I also took several courses in sales and marketing, which have helped a lot in this job.

You mention talk that we're involved in some merger negotiations out west. Of course we're always open to new ideas, but rumors are not reality. And yes, our earnings are an incentive for any good agency to want to join us. No, no. I'm not going to mention names. All I'll admit is that I did call a press conference this morning at which I released unaudited quarterly earnings figures showing a 16 percent rise over last year. The questions were hot and heavy. I emphasized that I didn't necessarily expect earnings to be up 16 percent for the year as a whole. The precise quote was that I saw "growth over the rest of the year consistent with the success of the first quarter, all else being equal."

Everyone wanted to know if this was pre-merger propaganda. Like I'm going to say, "Yes, Bob. Good question. That's *exactly* what this is." I admit I'm trying to paint CME in the most positive light I can. But propaganda? What I said was something like, "results like those of our first quarter certainly are attractive to potential candidates for acquisition. And I have no reason to believe that any prospective mergers would dilute our earnings for the year. At CME we try to get it right one quarter at a time. Our long-term progress has been the result of successfully stitching together a long series of quarters."

Not much of a metaphor, I guess. But I made my point. You can't tell people everything in this job. But you definitely have to make sure that what you *do* say is not untrue. Not only because, you know, it's the right thing to do. But also because with all the 10b-5 suits being filed these days against public companies, a slight misstatement may trigger a shareholder's claim that I was, or we were, hiding information. So I've got to be accurate. I pride myself on that....

Claire Monte, Confidential Log
April 19
Best I can think of is to keep my mouth shut and try to rally the troops. Sent a formal letter yesterday to Herb Ailing, reminding him of the consequences if he accuses us of something he can't back up in court.

Meantime, I've called Al Kim over at Kim & Biederman and told him to get the Wright Brothers to sign on the dotted line as soon as possible. Yesterday, preferably. And I've got some of my people here scrambling to put together a history of our consolidation software so we can start to figure out where we stand. Didn't tell them why, of course. Said I was interested in maybe working up some internal publicity, or even rewarding some of the folks who developed the software. My only hope is that Ailing doesn't know how close we are with Wright Brothers. I got the feeling from talking to him that he was under the impression we were still just thinking about Chicago. But we're almost there, goddammit. Just a few more days.

Memo from Asher Rippon to Claire Monte
April 20
As you asked, I've set up a meeting this afternoon (3:00 p.m., Conference Room D) on the subject of the development of our accounting consolidation software. Fortunately, I was able to reach Mike Weiss in Aspen. He's going to hold this afternoon free and we'll conference him into our meeting. He says that when he left CME, he transferred all of his notes and development documents to storage. I've sent for the whole package for the years you indicated and it should be here tomorrow morning.

Should you or I talk to Scoop Reymund? He's been around forever as I understand it and according to Weiss may have some insights on development of the system.

By the way, I've prepared the release about our merger agreement with Wright Brothers and everything looks good. I'm hearing some weird rumors, though. This morning Mary Kate Nakamura of the *Journal* was on the phone, asking me about a potential copyright infringement claim by Maxico. I said what kind of infringement and she either didn't know or wouldn't tell me. I know Mary Kate and was able to convince her the rumors were bogus, but if that's what this software stuff is all about, you've got to let me know. Our shares are up another point on speculation about the merger, but if word gets out we're hiding news of a claim, we're asking for serious trouble.

See you this afternoon.

Claire Monte, Confidential Log
April 21
Just as I suspected. Ailing knows what's going on and wants us to call off negotiations with Wright Brothers before he'll even think of talking over the infringement claim. Got my best people working on the system history, trying to figure out if there's anything to the claim but so far no answers. Asher Rippon is on to me, wants me to announce the possible litigation to protect us from shareholder suits but I just can't do it. We're so close with Wright Brothers, the bank's already on board and Alan Kim promised me he'd get a signature today in Chicago. Don't know what's got the Wrights so skittish all of a sudden. So far Asher's doing a good job keeping the rumors at bay and I wish I could tell him everything but can't. Not yet.

The Wall Street Journal, April 24
By Mary Kate Nakamura
Several days of speculation ended today when New York City's Maxico, Inc. filed a $44 million copyright infringement suit against Memphis-based holding company Consolidated Media Enterprises (CME). By the end of trading Friday, CME stock had fallen 9 points from $43.50 to $34.50, reflecting industry concerns that CME earnings estimates for the year are too high in light of the new claim....

The Wall Street Journal, June 19
By Mary Kate Nakamura
Attorney Joseph Markewiecz today announced the filing of a $9 million dollar shareholders' suit against Memphis-based Consolidated Media Enterprises (CME) for what he termed "deception, chicanery, and double-talk" in the company's alleged withholding of information from shareholders in the wake of a copyright infringement claim brought by rival Maxico, Inc. against CME in April of this year.

Mr. Markewiecz said his claim was based on Section 10b-5 of the Securities Exchange Act of 1934, which forbids any "manipulation or deceptive device...in connection with the purchase or sale of a security."

Spokesman Martin Najarian, who replaced long-time CME spokesman Asher Rippon following Mr. Rippon's well-publicized departure earlier this month, had no comment on the filing.

Reaction:

_____

_____

_____

_____

_____

_____

_____

_____

_____

_____

_____

_____

_____

Lonely at the Bottom, Too

The conscientious reader will no doubt have recognized several flaws in Claire Monte's decision-making process. There is obviously a large component of self-interest—to Monte, after all, CME and Claire Monte are almost indistinguishable—bound up in our protagonist's view of events. Yet she doesn't even try to distance herself from the issue. Because she's so concerned with secrecy, she hamstrings her own attempt to ascertain all the facts concerning the development of CME's software. In her obsession with a short-term organizational goal, she is letting the timing of events control her. She hasn't bothered to consult with anyone, and as a result lacks a clear understanding of the risks involved for those affected by her conduct.

But perhaps the biggest flaw in Claire Monte's decision-making is that she fails, finally, to make a clear-cut decision at all. It doesn't count to say that failing to decide is itself a sort of decision. What is needed here is the right *kind* of decision: one that is openly arrived at, benefits from the advice and data available from others, and is communicated to others affected by and involved in the deliberations.

Let's look at Monte's actions from our three familiar perspectives. Has she acted pragmatically in letting the tide of events carry CME along as she hoped for the Wright Brothers deal to close? Isn't there anything to be said for her tight-lipped approach? How was she to know, after all, whether Herb Ailing was playing from strength? And why let rumors run wild if they could possibly be avoided? Maybe if the Maxico claim had proved to be nothing more than a scare tactic, Monte would now be congratulating herself on her composure.

Even assuming, though, that there is some justification for Monte's indecision, at what point does this justification crumble? Is it when Monte realizes that there might be something *to* the Maxico allegations? When Asher Rippon calls a press conference to plug the performance of CME stock? When the Wright Brothers begin to balk at the deal—spooked, perhaps, by rumors on the Street?

At any rate, the final result of Monte's failure to act decisively and openly is decidedly unpragmatic. Maxico's lawsuit would have been filed in any case. But there are other considerations: The loss of a merger opportunity which might, with candor, merely have been postponed or repriced.

Damage to CME's reputation for forthrightness. Additional damage (above and beyond what would have been caused by Maxico's lawsuit anyway) to shareholders who might have bought their first, or additional, shares after Asher Rippon's cheerleading press conference. A lawsuit by angry shareholders. And internal damage to CME, as evidenced by Asher Rippon's defection from the company following Maxico's filing.

How, if at all, has Claire Monte acted *fairly* through all of this? How has she acted with respect for the interests and rights of others? The group of "others" that springs to mind first, of course, is CME's shareholders. But what about CME's management, directors, and employees? Have their rights to a reputation for sincerity been compromised? So what if they have? Is this something for a manager—not necessarily a financial manager, but *any* manager—to worry about?

Finally: What would you have done differently? And when would you have done it?

Chapter 14

Picking Up the Pieces: **Dealing With Bad Decisions** **(1995)**

How much goodness can be forced on a person?

Decisions have a wildly varying range of consequences and half-lives. Sometimes we're not around long enough to see the consequences of our own. Other times we have to live with choices other people have made. What we find is that the consequences of a course of action can go deeper than what we see.

Values and the Volume Seller

Impact Securities was founded as a NYSE wirehouse broker in 1965 by Milt Harris and Gaylord Belmont, formerly the two top producers in E.F. Hutton's west coast office. In 1974, having established a quietly successful operation in Los Angeles, Harris and Belmont moved their headquarters to New York and eventually made a public offering of their stock. The company sponsored the Impact Money Market Reserve Fund for its own customers and, as the decade went on, established itself as a broker of small-bank certificates of deposit, which were generally federally insured.

In the '80s, Impact expanded its sales of insurance annuities, building a geographically diversified client base of retirees, and with its new investment banking department became a banker for the commercial paper of corporations needing bridge loans for prospective mergers. As its business expanded, Impact created a family of mutual funds to compete with the popular independent funds, achieving slow but steady growth in that booming market. This was the situation in the early part of this decade, when the company underwent some very dramatic changes—as evidenced by the following tape-recorded material.

Oral History Entry
9/19/91
Perk Snyder. Hello? As you— *Hello? Are we rolling?* Okay. This is Perk Snyder speaking. As you know, I've been CEO at Impact for almost three months. I want to talk a little bit today about my vision for the future and how we're starting to move toward that. Milt Harris, my predecessor, and one of the founders of Impact, was very big on this oral history project and I don't want to disappoint him. Of course by the time anyone listens to this, you'll know how it all worked out anyway, but what the hey.

I've completed phase one by reorganizing our mutual funds department. Costs had gone up and we were starting to feel a little uneasy about making our budget numbers. My solution was to develop alternative compensation systems on fund sales and more efficient ways of investing for the fund, such as consolidating the cash reserves of the Impact Growth Fund with those of our Small Company Fund. Result: cost savings increased our performance numbers, and sales have gone up, but our total profits are still flat.

I started with Impact in New York 15 years ago and never felt any sentimental ties to the L.A. operation. Not like Milt, who started out on the Coast and hightailed it back there as soon as he handed over the reins to me here in Manhattan. I would never criticize him for his support of Carol Rubato as manager out there. She's always done a good job in terms of relationship selling, which appealed to Milt, who cut his teeth on that sort of thing. But that isn't where the firm is at right now. My group grew up where the competition is, in trading. That's how we were tested and identified as winners.

I wanted to move cautiously, but was unsatisfied with the limited contribution the West Coast was making to overall firm profits. I was motivated by my job definition and the profit goals, sure, but I also wanted our people out there to be part of the team, sharing in the success of the firm as contributors and as beneficiaries. And the time was right. I still had the new-chief momentum.

In early September I went to the three members of the Operations Oversight Committee of the Board, two of them independent directors who had served on the Nominating Committee that selected me. I told them about my disappointment with the sleepwalkers out west and their negative effects on our overall growth. I said that as a public company— as a company, that is, with shareholders breathing down our neck—we needed to prepare an up-to-date analysis of the western operations, and a plan to improve them.

The OOC passed its enthusiasm on at the Board luncheon, formally proposing that I spearhead a company-wide analysis for the Committee as soon as possible. At the end of the meeting, while the Board was still present, I got Milt on the horn and said that the Board had just been discussing the latest financials. Milt said to the crowd, "Don't be discouraged, fellas. Our people out here are very loyal and that sort of support is beyond price." As he hung up, I grinned at the Board and said, "Only problem with that advice is that too many of Milt's loyal customers don't pay us one red cent."

Two weeks later, I submitted the following executive summary:

> To The Operations Oversight Committee
> PERSONAL AND CONFIDENTIAL
> 1. You have asked me to review the financials and trace out the reasons for the recent flattening in our profit margins.

2. Impact boasts some undeniable strengths as we move from a national to a global presence. For one thing, we haven't made the mistake of many other firms in constructing our own version of the Taj Mahal as headquarters. We've always been at the forefront in utilizing computer technology. We've appointed consultants as local agents in a lot of good locations and had high-level talent available when new opportunities came up. Yet based on our customer base, we haven't done as well as we might.

3. Our problem isn't losses, simply unsatisfactory growth. And the problem isn't new. Looking back—and this is not to criticize anyone—it's easy to see how our customer base in the west has generated flat-line revenues while our overall costs have risen. The L.A. office has had a free ride and in many cases failed to participate in our most profitable products, with the end result that they, and we, have lost a number of investment opportunities.

4. The Why is that the L.A. sales staff doesn't do sales. They're a bunch of Lana Turners. Not for them to drum up customer interest in new products. They're waiting to be discovered. Getting them to GO should be Carol Rubato's job, but I just don't see it happening. Admittedly, she's a very good accountant and compliance officer. And Milt

in his day thought of her as a strong right arm. But her attitude sends a strange signal to the sales force, whom she insists, contrary to our practice here in New York, on calling customer service representatives.

The bottom line is that not one of our L.A. people generates the numbers of even our worst New York rep. Carol lets this happen, and it's the wrong signal, as far as I'm concerned. There's simply no incentive for anyone to make moves. For example, those customers pay us a small fee for holding their stocks. This is a loss leader for us, but no one dares to mention it. As a result, the customers don't feel guilty leaving their stocks untouched year after year, with us producing the tax records while the dividends flow right out to them. And, competing with our own products, I know for a fact that our people often suggest that the customers handle some of their own certificates of deposit. All right, not one of them got burned when the S&Ls were shaken up. But they were certainly close to the fire, and the reps let them put their CD money into local banks the particular customers had personal contact with.

Sure, they kept the customers, but why bother? I find this sort of conduct very unprofessional, considering we have a broad line of CD products ourselves. And definitely a bad precedent. Not surprisingly, when our employees don't help in the security offerings we take on, the customers don't hear about them. But I don't blame the reps. A lot of them are good. Just misdirected, and—I hate to say it—mismanaged.

5. Other western operations run out of L.A. barely break even with travel expenses. The distances out there are enormous, and there don't seem to be many discount fares from LAX to Glenwood Springs, Eureka, and Provo.

6. Milt seems to be happy out west. Pleasant people for him to talk to and no history of complaining customers. We all respect Milt and we obviously owe him a lot. But we can't treat L.A. as a hobby. Impact is a profit-making operation and my job is to make it more so. We say our corporate values are:

> *Be Tough*
> *Be Excited*
> *Be a Team*

Call me sentimental, but I agree with each of these goals. Our game plan works in New York. We need to see it in the west as well. L.A. has to be brought into sync.

NOTE: Charts illustrating several of the above points are attached.

Oral History Entry
10/7/93
Perk Snyder. Um, hello. I don't have much time, but this is a brief update of the firm's status, and a report on what's been going on around here.

The short answer is, Impact Securities has never been better. I was just listening to my last entry, so I suppose I ought to start where I left off. By the time my memo got to the Executive Committee, everyone was all worked up. In our detailed discussions, I clamped a tight lid on the project. There was serious risk of damage to the firm if word leaked out that major management changes were even being discussed. People might have started to jump ship. I figured we might have to push a few people when the time came, but I didn't want to see anyone jumping.

I really enjoy controlling my own work, and the CIA type of process made it even more fun. There were no detailed fact-finding reports, no boring consulting sessions. To cut a long story short, I was given the go-ahead on my plan to increase west coast support for Impact products by lighting a fire under our L.A. reps. I felt like we needed new and aggressive management, and I replaced Carol Rubato with my old buddy Red Rogers the same day I heard back from the Board.

Red had carte blanche on getting the L.A. office up to speed with the rest of the firm. After testing them for a couple of months, we added a series of focused bonus plans for sales, using a low base—last year's results and last year's customers—to measure our progress against. Red dumped the dead wood, the people who couldn't sell mice to a mamba, and brought on some hotshots from a couple of other firms in the city. By July of this year, our West Coast numbers were up 17%.

Because of the distances to be covered and the limited number of people available to cover them, I'm now testing gypsy offices out in the hinterlands. The idea is just to set up some local, maybe a housewife, or a realtor, to man a phone and be available to pass out our sales stuff. The point is not for the gypsy to do any actual selling, only to get people interested. Then I've assigned all the L.A. personnel secondary territories. They get names from the gypsies, then call or fly out to meet with the prospective clients. So we get local representation with none of the hassle of examinations and registrations.

Maybe my best idea, and something we're still working hard on, is to provide a drawing card for getting our name out to prospective customers. That drawing card is Cale Cullen. Thanks to a little creative bookkeeping on our part, Cale's got a record similar to Peter Lynch or Nicholas Bratt, and hey, he's about a hundred times better looking to boot. So we fly him around to sign copies of his book and give investment seminars, and it's really starting to pay off. He pushes the benefits for retail customers of a flexible mutual fund structure like we have, along with the availability of continuing support from our

L.A. office. We've set him up in Jackson Hole, so he plays it all as a hometown boy, showing up for a movie or a meeting in Denver or Cheyenne, shaking a few hands, grinning a lot. A real star. We even make a profit on his video!

As for—hmm. I'm looking at my notes here. As for Carol Rubato, we offered her early retirement, the title of Advisor to the President, and a retainer for three years. Plus a new electronic office at home so she wouldn't get in Red's way. Tied her long-range retirement to the growth of West Coast profits. She didn't complain when she saw the golden handshake. And the headline in the Impact *Lance* (that was my idea, changing the name of the old *Chronicle* to the *Lance*, to reflect our new ethos) read "Gold in Them Thar Hills," with the story expressing pride in the strong foundation Carol established during her tenure as manager and in the loyalty, professionalism, and flexibility of her staff. *Et cetera, et cetera.*

Milt Harris has never really jumped on the bus. He's been smart enough not to interfere, but I know he's watching me closely. Especially with a few of these customer complaints we've gotten recently. Nothing big: just a couple of retirees grousing about costs they claim we didn't tell them were coming. I told Milt that every company, from Merrill Lynch on down, gets that sort of thing. He didn't seem satisfied. Tough. I hope he'll get on board eventually. Because if not, we're going to leave without him. I've got everyone saying it now:

> *Be Tough*
> *Be Excited*
> *Be a Team*

Oral History Entry
3/22/95
Aeneas Brown. Testing. Testing. Okay. I'm, uh—
Let me introduce myself first. This is Aeneas Brown,
since early February the new CEO of Impact
Securities. I just want to get this whole oral history
thing restarted, partly at the behest of Milt Harris,
who set it up in the first place and was religious
about making monthly entries, and partly to
memorialize for myself what's been happening with
the company lately.

First of all, Perk Snyder is gone. Milt Harris flexed
his muscles as one of the firm's largest stockholders
and rounded up a few likeminded folks to vote out
the directors who backed Perk. The reasons were
pretty obvious. Cale Cullen left the firm to start his
own group of funds, and later called Impact a
"smallminded bunch of car salesmen." It wouldn't
have been so bad, except he did it on the Larry King
Show. Then he held up his latest book. Over the
course of the next month we lost something like $11
million from our funds. Investors following the Pied
Piper, I guess. Perk Snyder wanted a star. He got
one. Just not a very grateful one.

We're also dealing with an ongoing SEC investigation
of Perk's use of unregistered gypsy consultants out
west, and at last count 12 private damage suits based

on alleged misrepresentations made by our brokers in L.A. On the whole, I'd have to say things have looked better for Impact.

I can't say I was enthusiastic about taking this job. I did it primarily out of loyalty to Milt Harris, who was a classmate of my mother's at Claremont and has been a family friend ever since. In a sense you could say that his life's work went down the tube while Perk played three-card monte with the customers. As I understood the Board's offer of the CEO position, I could play a timely role, come in like Walter Cronkite, fatherly, with no axes to grind, and maybe settle things down.

I suppose it was wise to bring in an outsider. The fact is, I really *don't* have any axes to grind. Not even one to bury in Perk Snyder. But I had a litigator friend who worked for Judge Ansel Lumbard. Will must have reminded me a hundred times of the gospel according to Lumbard: "Never assume a goddamned thing." Well, it seems to me that Perk assumed an awful lot when he framed The Question facing the firm as: "How do we turn the West Coast office into a group of successful sellers of east coast products?"

Given Impact's current problems, I have to assume that Perk's big question was wrong. Impact has to make a profit, yes. But it has to do so in a way that meshes with our customers' needs and risk-taking capacity. So maybe the question is how to identify and meet the needs of the West Coast customers. Or how to build a stronger customer base there.

We learn in business school that marketing is more than just making a sale. Selling is a part of the process, yes, but only a part. The process begins with research of a market's preferences and characteristics. With your study results in hand, you look at the needs, objectives, aspirations, and financial capacity of your prospective customers. At the same time, you think about and modify existing products. Modify them, consider the distribution channels, and maybe create new ones. Then you deal with sales, actual and expected. And as that process proceeds and the circle is completed, you look again at your prospective customers' needs, refining your data in light of all this information as the circle is repeated. It may sound like Sisyphus, but in fact every cycle is different.

Here in management the process is continuous, too. By the time a decision has been made and is being implemented, you start scratching your head about what's been learned, about how the answer and the process of getting there can be improved and brought into the corporate memory for the next tough decision.

But at some level the task facing us now isn't simply a matter of tactics. It's more a matter of soul.

In the Funds we've moved already to upgrade the importance and authority of outside directors as representing the shareholders as well as the management company's needs.

In the company itself, I want to shake people up. Get them to start thinking about our clients as people again, not just as opponents. Not just as prey. I'd like to dust off Impact's old statement of purpose and post it on the walls around here. And what about requiring peer approval for recommendation of any purchase of a below-investment-grade security? What about requiring our brokers to advise their customers of their right to get what they say in *writing*? If voluntary compliance isn't working, I may go the other route—install computer programs to pick up possible ethical problems in our trading and put up the red flag for further investigation.

I'm also talking about reminders and mottos, names on a Person of the Month poster, having a special parking spot for the week. Sounds stupid, I know. Welcome to the Robert Fulghum School of Business Management, right? Motto:

> *Who are we?*
> *Where are we going?*
> *How 'bout a hug?*

But hey, it's still better than that fascist mantra Perk Snyder used to have everyone chant. The fact is, we're going somewhere else from here, and we're going to need every imaginable credible external reinforcement. We're going to have to reach beyond management and get everyone to buy in on the mission. It's not just a matter of compliance with the regs. That's the baseline, not our goal. We're going to have to pick and choose among the detritus that Perk left behind to build a new house, finding some basic principles which engage us individually and as an organization.

To get there, we need to single out the people who practice what we preach. I've rechristened our company newsletter *Mutual Interest*, and plan to use it to publicize our best employees. I've put out the word that we want all of our people to join the relevant professional organizations—the Analysts' Society, the Institute of Certified Financial Planners— and look to their codes of ethics for guidance in their careers with us. Listed the new members and the old. Permitted and encouraged all employees to take up to five hours off each month to do community service, and asked our Human Resources staff to publicize their stories in the newsletter.

I once worked with a very ethical firm in San Francisco. It never made much of that fact, taking the position that calling attention to one's virtues was itself unvirtuous. I've tried to keep that in mind as to the outside world here at Impact, in order to answer the likely suspicion that we have an ulterior motive in all this ethics stuff.

When I turned down a chance to do the bridge financing for one of the Japanese multinationals involved in deforesting New Guinea, our crowd began to believe. I realize there's a risk that I'll be laughed at on the Street. That people are going to think I'm not tough enough to keep the firm in the black. In fact, two of our vice-presidents left when

I turned down the Japanese. But one of those who stayed on told me she stayed because for the first time in her career, she was proud to be working here.

So am I.

Reaction:

_____

_____

_____

_____

_____

_____

_____

_____

_____

_____

_____

_____

_____

_____

Exegesis

In what sense, if any, is Aeneas Brown an improvement over Perk Snyder? There are some obvious answers. First off, he wants to make sure Impact complies with the applicable securities regulations. That's probably a good thing. He's concerned about Impact's customers. He's even concerned about Impact's employees.

But is there anything about his plans for Impact that disturbs you? Put another way, how much goodness can be forced on a person? What if, as an employee, you didn't *want* to do community service on a regular basis? What if you didn't care to have the corporate credo hanging in your office? What if, frankly, you'd rather be left alone to make your own decisions?

All of this is to introduce the idea that we as individuals all function in environments, which are made up not only of walls and floors and potted plants but also of other people, and other people's values, and other people's decisions. Perk Snyder's profiteering Impact was probably a less desirable place to work than Aeneas Brown's kinder, gentler firm will be. And yet Brown's vision contains its own nascent problems. In his determination to do the right thing, he is, for example, assuming that he knows what the right thing *is*—and that his employees and officers and shareholders will share the belief.

To return one final time to our ethical categories, Brown is trying hard to do justice through his guidance of Impact. But is he being pragmatic? How ethical can a company be? And who decides what its ethics are?

I realize that cautioning the reader about a securities firm that may be too ethically ambitious seems like a repudiation of everything we've covered so far. Again, I don't mean to criticize Brown. What I do mean to say is that decisions about right or wrong are always going to come down to the individual. Helpful as they undoubtedly are, laudatory newsletters and strategically placed statements of principles don't protect us from the pressure to make bad decisions. In fact, nothing protects us. The determinants of responsible behavior—intelligence, guts, real concern for the things we want to define us—are just as important in the good firm as they are in the bad.

Conclusion

The main thing is...you've got to be able to live with yourself. How many of these situations are going to be career makers or breakers? If it is a clear-cut career breaker, then, in my opinion, you need to re-think whether that's the kind of organization you want to be in.

Young manager
Quoted in "Business Ethics:
A View From the Trenches,"
by Joseph L. Badaracco, Jr.
and Allen P. Webb

Chapter 15

Practicing Spiritual Sabotage:
A Beginning

*And if you can't? If the pressure to cheapen yourself
continues?*

By now the dedicated reader of *Values Added* has suffered
through the dithering of a long parade of cretins and
flops. Let me just say before proceeding that I've known
only a few of these people in my several decades working
on Wall Street. My colleagues have generally been intelligent
men and women of outstanding integrity. I've been proud
to work with them in the most exciting environment I can
imagine—the financial markets that have fueled this country's
phenomenal growth and ascent to power. I wouldn't trade
the experience for anything.

There's a reason for a book full of boobs. Bad decisions
make good reading. We can often learn more laughing than
crying. But the truth is that the vast majority of decisions
made every day in American markets are made correctly, if
not always deliberately.

So why a book on ethics in the financial marketplace? Because any look in the newspaper will reveal the details of another exception to the rule. Another illegal trade. Another astonishing Ponzi scheme.

What's seen less often is the human cost. Financiers flame out. Brokers cop pleas, and bond traders put bullets through their own heads. Anyone who's made a living in finance can tell you why. It's absorbing, often triumphant work, but it's work that can eat the soul. The chief threats to individual character arise from the intimidation of an impersonal, often ruthless workplace and the seductive bait, dangled at the same time, of personal financial security. The latter can make the former seem worthwhile for far too long.

Eat the Young

The pressures start immediately. The scholars Joseph L. Badaracco, Jr. and Allen P. Webb published in 1995 the results of a survey of 30 recent graduates of the Harvard MBA program, many of whom have already been asked to compromise. Badaracco and Webb found that:

> The young managers believed, in effect, that the people who pressured them to act in sleazy ways were responding to four powerful organizational commandments. First, performance is what really counts, so make your numbers. Second, be loyal and show us that you're a team player. Third, don't break the law. Fourth, don't over-invest in ethical behavior. Taken by themselves, the first three commandments are hardly immoral. But while they are almost certainly necessary for a successful

organization, they are hardly sufficient for creating
an ethical or responsible one, especially when a fourth
powerful norm encourages sleazy behavior.

Creating an atmosphere in which principled conduct can
flourish is difficult work. It's not just a matter of official
pronouncement or corporate creed, though each of these is
a good start. It's also important to recognize responsible
behavior among one's colleagues, whether through formal
award or citation or simply through verbal praise, increasing
responsibility, and professional advancement. Conversely,
senior managers have to rid themselves of colleagues who
can't or won't act responsibly, whether those colleagues are
Rusty Merrick or Philip Granada, Nicholas Leeson or Dennis
Levine.

But what if they don't? What if your employer or your
colleagues simply don't *care* about encouraging ethical
behavior? What do you do when you're asked to
compromise, to lie, to manipulate? Perhaps, as our 7-step
template suggests, you need to get a good hold of the facts.
See how others react to the boss. Identify the effects of the
abusive behavior. Who's being hurt? How badly? If *you're*
the one who's being hurt, can you hold out long enough to
move up, or out? Are there any alternatives? Commandment
#4 in the Badaracco quadrilogue supports the boss: *Don't
overinvest in ethics.* But #3 is *Don't do anything illegal.*
From that angle, might you be able to reposition the problem
by getting some reinforcement from the legal department?
Maybe you could even save the boss from an embarrassing
gaffe.

And if you can't? If the pressure to cheapen yourself
continues? I personally believe that few means of self-defense
are unjustified in this sort of situation. Consider the

description by Michael Lewis of a day at work at Salomon Brothers and the dicey on-line-in-the-financial markets problem he faced. It takes a reading of his book *Liar's Poker* to get the full fragrance of the abusive atmosphere around him, but the Just Do It order he describes in the book's final chapter is a pretty good proxy.

Junk bonds were a new priority for Salomon, which needed to sell massive amounts of debt to pay off a bridge loan extended by it and another investment bank to Southland Corporation, owners of the 7-11 chain of convenience stores. The junk bond department would earn $30 million dollars in profits if the deal succeeded. Lewis's instinct was that the bonds were overpriced and that he should stick with his New Year's resolution to stop selling people things he didn't think they should buy. His challenge was how to steer his customers around the bonds. Deluged by calls from his anxious New York managers, Lewis replied that he was giving it his best shot when in fact he hadn't placed a single sales call. Finally, a specialist insisted on watching while Lewis pitched his biggest client. The conversation included the following dialogue:

> *Lewis:* There is a deal you should look at... It's extremely popular with American investors. *(The client was a contrarian—and not high on Americans.)*
> *Client:* Then we should let them buy it all.
> *Lewis:* I'm sitting here with one of our high-yield bond specialists, who thinks Southland bonds are cheap.
> *Client:* But you don't.
> *Lewis:* Right! *(Launching into an extended sales pitch.)*
> *Client:* No, thanks.

Lewis carried through by writing *Liar's Poker* and giving up bonds altogether. You may simply want to shift employers. A firm with disrespect for principled behavior— a latter-day Drexel Burnham Lambert, for example—isn't going to be around long anyway. So save yourself. Insist on your own integrity. We all believe in something. Don't let your job or your boss or your bank account take it away. Shout your beliefs. In Christ. In Allah. In every redwood that ever dwarfed a dumptruck. Hector. Plead. Embarrass yourself. Inhumanity thrives in silence, and darkness, and conformity. If you think your voice is being ignored, move on. Find a company that values the same things you do. Honesty, for one. Collegiality. A commitment to bettering the world, even if only in very small increments.

Those, anyway, are the values I would like to abide by. What are yours? Are they workable? Can you keep them?

And can you apply them?

The End

Appendix

The International Organization of Securities Commissions International Conduct of Business Principles

A limited number of comments have been added to individual principles, where the working party believed it would be useful to illustrate the principle by reference to some rules or obligations which might fall within its boundaries.

1. HONESTY AND FAIRNESS

In conducting its business activities, a firm should act honestly and fairly in the best interests of its customers and the integrity of the market.

Comment: This principle includes any obligation to avoid misleading and deceptive acts or representations.

2. DILIGENCE

In conducting its business activities, a firm should act with due skill, care and diligence, in the best interests of its customers and the integrity of the market.

Comment: This principle includes any duty of best execution.

3. CAPABILITIES

A firm should have and employ effectively the resources and procedures which are needed for the proper performance of its business activities.

Comment: This principle includes any obligation for the firm
            to have and implement effectively rules and internal
            procedures for its employees and representatives
            to make sure that they comply with these principles,
            including staff dealing rules.

4. *INFORMATION ABOUT CUSTOMERS*

A firm should seek from its customers information about
their financial situation, investment experience and
investment objectives relevant to the services to be provided.

Comments: This principle includes any obligation to "know
            one's customer." This principle is a necessary
            element in enabling the firm to fulfill any suitability
            requirements.

5. *INFORMATION FOR CUSTOMERS*

A firm should make adequate disclosure of relevant
material information in its dealings with its customers.

Comments: This principle includes any obligation of the firm:
            • to acquire and provide information, including
            information about risks, needed by the customer to
            make informed investment decisions;
            • to provide timely and accurate reports to the
            customer about business undertaken for or with the
            customer.

6. *CONFLICTS OF INTEREST*

A firm should try to avoid conflicts of interest, and when
they cannot be avoided, should ensure that its customers are
fairly treated.

Comment: This principle recognizes that conflicts of interests of interest may be managed, and that proper management to ensure fair treatment of customers may require disclosure, internal rules of confidentiality, or other appropriate methods or combinations of methods.

7. COMPLIANCE

A firm should comply with all regulatory requirements applicable to the conduct of its business activities so as to promote the best interests of customers and the integrity of the market.

IOSCO adopted its International Conduct of Business Principles in 1990. Member countries were directed in turn to adopt the Principles and implementing rules, using text appropriate to their local situations. For further information write to the

Office of the Secretary General
800 Square Victoria, Suite 4210,
Postal Box 171,
Montreal, H4Z 1C8, Canada;

or go to their web site at

http://www.iosco.org

Merrill Lynch Principles

Our corporate culture at Merrill Lynch is the sum total of what we believe and think, how we work together as colleagues and how we conduct ourselves as individuals.

It is the way we treat our clients, our shareholders, our fellow employees, our neighbors and the public in general.

It is *who we are*.

And while our corporate culture is by nature indefinable, it begins and ends with certain principles that underlie our success as a business and as individuals.

Our future growth and prosperity depend on our continued commitment to these principles and our ability to instill them in others.

Client Focus

Our clients are the driving force behind what we do.

Our company's founder, Charles E. Merrill, declared that the client's interests must come first. Today, client focus is just as imperative as it was in Mr. Merrill's day. In our increasingly competitive industry, success rests not on our ability to sell a certain product or service, but on the degree to which clients value Merrill Lynch as their trusted adviser.

To achieve this stature, it will not be enough merely to meet our clients' expectations. We must constantly strive to exceed them.

Respect for the Individual

We respect the dignity of each individual, whether an employee, shareholder, client or member of the general public.

We strive to be a lean, decisive and aggressive organization, but on a personal level to treat each individual with dignity, consideration and respect. This means sharing the credit when credit is due, avoiding public criticism of one another, and encouraging an atmosphere in which openness, cooperation and mutual consultation are the norms. It means following the Golden Rule.

As a company, we will seek, nurture and reward the highest-caliber employees, regardless of race, national origin, religion, gender, age or physical ability. We will encourage this diversity amongst ourselves, realizing it to be an important competitive advantage in the rapidly emerging global marketplace.

Teamwork

We strive for seamless integration of services. In our clients' eyes, there is only one Merrill Lynch.

It is great teams that win, not loose affiliations of all-stars. Therefore, we expect real teamwork throughout our company, and we reward people for it. We are committed to an honest sharing of both risks and rewards with one another, so that when clients achieve their goals, everyone at Merrill Lynch benefits.

Our people and resources are unmatched in our industry, yet they are not enough to guarantee continued success. In order to be our clients' trusted adviser, we must take pride in working as a team—at all levels and across all boundaries—bringing all of the diverse skills and resources of Merrill Lynch to bear in solving client problems.

Responsible Citizenship

As the company that brought Wall Street to Main Street and the world, we seek to improve the quality of life in the communities where our employees live and work.

Responsible citizenship means that we are committed to giving something back to the communities in which we earn our livelihood. We encourage employee volunteerism and community involvement. Both as a corporation and as individuals, we support education, the cultural arts, the environment and community services in the U.S. and around the world.

And, we advocate public policies—such as open global markets and enhanced incentives for savings and investment—that promote long-term economic growth and opportunity around the world.

Integrity

No one's personal bottom line is more important than the reputation of our firm.

Our most important corporate asset is the great Merrill Lynch "tradition of trust"—our company's long-standing reputation for integrity in the marketplace.

As beneficiaries of this great tradition, we will be tolerant of ordinary mistakes made in the course of business; we will not tolerate lapses in ethics or integrity.

While "R.O.I." does not appear on our financial statements, Merrill Lynch enjoys a return on integrity that we will protect, whatever the cost, as the bedrock of our prosperity and our pride.

© 1993 Merrill Lynch & Co., Inc. The Principles are published, taught, and discussed in Merrill Lynch offices throughout the world. Our thanks to the firm for permission to publish in *Values Added* their complete text. Further information is available at the Merrill Lynch web site: http://www.ml.doc

The Caux Round Table

*In a world which is experiencing profound transforma-
tions, the Caux Round Table of business leaders from Europe,
Japan and the United States is committed to energizing the
role of business and industry as a vital force for innovative
global change.*

*The Round Table was founded in 1986 by Frederik
Philips, former President of Philips Electronics, and Olivier
Giscard d'Estaing, Vice-Chairman of INSEAD, as a means
of reducing escalating trade tensions. It is concerned with
the development of constructive economic and social
relationships between the participants' countries, and with
their urgent joint responsibilities toward the rest of the world.*

*At the urging of Ryuzaburo Kaku, Chairman of Canon
Inc., the Round Table has focused attention on the importance
of global corporate responsibility in reducing social and
economic threats to world peace and stability. The Round
Table recognizes that shared leadership is indispensable to
a revitalized and more harmonious world. It emphasizes
the development of continuing friendship, understanding and
cooperation, based on a common respect for the highest
moral values and on responsible action by individuals in
their own spheres of influence.*

Principles for Business

Introduction

The Caux Round Table believes that the world business
community should play an important role in improving
economic and social conditions. As a statement of

aspirations, this document aims to express a world standard against which business behavior can be measured. We seek to begin a process that identifies shared values, reconciles differing values, and thereby develops a shared perspective on business behavior acceptable to and honored by all.

These principles are rooted in two basic ethical ideals: *kyosei* and human dignity. The Japanese concept of *kyosei* means living and working together for the common good — enabling cooperation and mutual prosperity to coexist with healthy and fair competition. "Human dignity" refers to the sacredness or value of each person as an end, not simply as a means to the fulfillment of others' purposes or even majority prescription.

The General Principles in Section 2 seek to clarify the spirit of *kyosei* and "human dignity," while the specific Stakeholder Principles in Section 3 are concerned with their practical application.

In its language and form, the document owes a substantial debt to *The Minnesota Principles*, a statement of business behavior developed by the Minnesota Center for Corporate Responsibility. The Center hosted and chaired the drafting committee, which included Japanese, European, and U.S. representatives.

Business behavior can affect relationships among nations and the prosperity and well-being of us all. Business is often the first contact between nations and, by the way in which it causes social and economic changes, has a significant impact on the level of fear or confidence felt by people worldwide. Members of the Caux Round Table place their first emphasis on putting one's own house in order, and on seeking to establish what is right rather than who is right.

SECTION 1. PREAMBLE

The mobility of employment, capital, products and technology is making business increasingly global in its transactions and its effects.

Laws and market forces are necessary but insufficient guides for conduct.

Responsibility for the policies and actions of business and respect for the dignity and interests of its stakeholders are fundamental.

Shared values, including a commitment to shared prosperity, are as important for a global community as for communities of smaller scale.

For these reasons, and because business can be a powerful agent of positive social change, we offer the following principles as a foundation for dialogue and action by business leaders in search of business responsibility. In so doing, we affirm the necessity for moral values in business decision making. Without them, stable business relationships and a sustainable world community are impossible.

SECTION 2. GENERAL PRINCIPLES

Principle 1. *The Responsibilities of Businesses: Beyond Shareholders Toward Stakeholders*
The value of a business to society is the wealth and employment it creates and the marketable products and

services it provides to consumers at a reasonable price commensurate with quality. To create such value, a business must maintain its own economic health and viability, but survival is not a sufficient goal.

Businesses have a role to play in improving the lives of all their customers, employees, and shareholders by sharing with them the wealth they have created. Suppliers and competitors as well should expect businesses to honor their obligations in a spirit of honesty and fairness. As responsible citizens of the local, national, regional and global communities in which they operate, businesses share a part in shaping the future of those communities.

Principle 2. *The Economic and Social Impact of Business: Toward Innovation, Justice and World Community*

Businesses established in foreign countries to develop, produce or sell should also contribute to the social advancement of those countries by creating productive employment and helping to raise the purchasing power of their citizens. Businesses also should contribute to human rights, education, welfare, and vitalization of the countries in which they operate.

Businesses should contribute to economic and social development not only in the countries in which they operate, but also in the world community at large, through effective and prudent use of resources, free and fair competition, and emphasis upon innovation in technology, production methods, marketing and communications.

Principle 3. *Business Behavior: Beyond the Letter of Law Toward a Spirit of Trust*

While accepting the legitimacy of trade secrets, businesses should recognize that sincerity, candor, truthfulness, the keeping of promises, and transparency contribute not only to their own credibility and stability but also to the smoothness and efficiency of business transactions, particularly on the international level.

Principle 4. *Respect for Rules*

To avoid trade frictions and promote freer trade, equal conditions for competition, and fair and equitable treatment for all participants, businesses should respect international and domestic rules. In addition, they should recognize that some behavior, although legal, may still have adverse consequences.

Principle 5. *Support for Multilateral Trade*

Businesses should support the multilateral trade systems of the GATT/World Trade Organization and similar international agreements. They should cooperate in efforts to promote the progressive and judicious liberalization of trade and to relax those domestic measures that unreasonably hinder global commerce, while giving due respect to national policy objectives.

Principle 6. *Respect for the Environment*

A business should protect and, where possible, improve the environment, promote sustainable development, and prevent the wasteful use of natural resources.

Principle 7. *Avoidance of Illicit Operations*

A business should not participate in or condone bribery, money laundering, or other corrupt practices: indeed, it should seek cooperation with others to eliminate them. It should not trade in arms or other materials used for terrorist activities, drug traffic or other organized crime.

SECTION 3. STAKEHOLDER PRINCIPLES

Customers

We believe in treating all customers with dignity, irrespective of whether they purchase our products and services directly from us or otherwise acquire them in the market. We therefore have a responsibility to:

- provide our customers with the highest quality products and services consistent with their requirements;
- treat our customers fairly in all aspects of our business transactions, including a high level of service and remedies for their dissatisfaction;
- make every effort to ensure that the health and safety of our customers, as well as the quality of their environment, will be sustained or enhanced by our products and services;
- assure respect for human dignity in products offered, marketing, and advertising; and
- respect the integrity of the culture of our customers.

Employees

We believe in the dignity of every employee and in taking employee interests seriously. We therefore have a responsibility to:

- provide jobs and compensation that improve workers' living conditions;
- provide working conditions that respect each employee's health and dignity;

- be honest in communications with employees and open in sharing information, limited only by legal and competitive constraints;
- listen to and, where possible, act on employee suggestions, ideas, requests and complaints;
- engage in good faith negotiations when conflict arises;
- avoid discriminatory practices and guarantee equal treatment and opportunity in areas such as gender, age, race and religion;
- promote in the business itself the employment of differently abled people in places of work where they can be genuinely useful;
- protect employees from avoidable injury and illness in the workplace;
- encourage and assist employees in developing relevant and transferable skills and knowledge; and
- be sensitive to the serious unemployment problems frequently associated with business decisions and work with governments, employee groups, other agencies and each other in addressing these dislocations.

Owners/Investors

We believe in honoring the trust our investors place in us. We therefore have a responsibility to:

- apply professional and diligent management in order to secure a fair and competitive return on our owners' investment;
- disclose relevant information to owners/investors subject only to legal requirements and competitive constraints;

- conserve, protect, and increase the owners'/ investors' assets; and
- respect owners'/investors' requests, suggestions, complaints and formal resolutions.

Suppliers

Our relationship with suppliers and subcontractors must be based on mutual respect. We therefore have a responsibility to:

- seek fairness and truthfulness in all of our activities, including pricing, licensing, and rights to sell;
- ensure that our business activities are free from coercion and unnecessary litigation;
- foster long-term stability in the supplier relationship in return for value, quality, competitiveness and reliability;
- share information with suppliers and integrate them into our planning processes;
- pay suppliers on time and in accordance with agreed terms of trade; and
- seek, encourage and prefer suppliers and subcontractors whose employment practices respect human dignity.

Competitors

We believe that fair economic competition is one of the basic requirements for increasing the wealth of nations and ultimately for making possible the just distribution of goods and services. We therefore have a responsibility to:

- foster open markets for trade and investment;
- promote competitive behavior that is socially and environmentally beneficial and demonstrates mutual respect among competitors;
- refrain from either seeking or participating in questionable payments or favors to secure competitive advantages;
- respect both tangible and intellectual property rights; and
- refuse to acquire commercial information by dishonest or unethical means, such as industrial espionage.

Communities

We believe that as global corporate citizens we can contribute to such forces of reform and human rights as are at work in the communities in which we operate. We therefore have a responsibility in those communities to:

- respect human rights and democratic institutions, and promote them wherever practicable;
- recognize government's legitimate obligation to the society at large and support public policies and practices that promote human development through harmonious relations between business and other segments of society;
- collaborate with those forces in the community dedicated to raising standards of health, education, workplace safety and economic well-being;
- promote and stimulate sustainable development and play a leading role in preserving and enhancing the physical environment and conserving the earth's resources;

- support peace, security, diversity and social integration;
- respect the integrity of local cultures; and
- be a good corporate citizen through charitable donations, educational and cultural contributions and employee participation in community and civic affairs.

©1994 Caux Round Table, an organization comprised of senior business leaders from Europe, Japan and the United States who are committed to energizing the role of business and industry as a vital force for innovative global change through principled business leadership.

We are most grateful for their permission to publish here the complete English version of the Principles for Business. For further information the Caux Round Table may be reached, in the United States, at 4626 France Avenue South, Minneapolis, Minnesota 55410.

Scudder, Stevens & Clark

Mission Statement

Our mission is to achieve a leadership position in global investment management by delivering value-added investment products and services to meet different investor requirements.

Our Goals

Set the standard of excellence for investment performance and service.
Attract, develop, and retain the most talented people for our business.
Develop and sustain our operational infrastructure as a source of competitive advantage.
Achieve a preeminent position in targeted markets.
Achieve a level of financial success that benefits our clients and employees.

Credo

We will at all times conduct ourselves with integrity and distinction, putting first the interests of our clients.

Scudder, Stevens & Clark, Inc. The Mission Statement, Goals and Credo are distributed, discussed and incorporated in long range planning as well as short term decision making throughout the firm. Policy and procedure memoranda and training sessions establish detailed guidelines for their implementation.

Our thanks to the firm for permission to include these benchmarks in *Values Added*. Further information is available from the firm's Public Relations Group at (212) 325-6753.

'Scudder, Stevens and Clark' and 'Scudder' are registered service marks of Scudder, Stevens and Clark, Inc.

New York Stock Exchange
Values/Behaviors

Integrity

Definition
- Acting with, and demanding in others, the highest standards of ethics, honesty and candor

Behaviors
- Demonstrates the highest level of honesty and ethical behavior
- Avoids real or apparent conflict of interest
- Communicates in a straightforward, candid and unpretentious manner
- Treats employees, customers and constituents fairly
- Works to foster the integrity of NYSE products and services
- Gives 100% effort on the job
- Demonstrates commitment to the integrity of the Exchange management system
- Encourages people to surface bad news as well as good news
- Challenges ideas that she/he believes are incorrect
- Strives to meet personal commitments
- Takes responsibility for her/his decisions (avoids blaming others)

Excellence

Definition
- Consistently achieving the highest quality performance in ourselves and expecting it in others

Behaviors
- Demonstrates personal commitment to high standards of quality performance
- Consistently works to improve group performance through team work
- Understands and supports the mission of the NYSE
- Makes sure objectives are clearly understood
- Consistently looks for better ways to get the job done
- Encourages and recognizes others' ideas
- Pays attention to details while keeping sight of overall objectives
- Meets deadlines
- Exhibits pride in the NYSE

Respect for the Individual

Definition
- Treating others with dignity and consideration

Behaviors
- Demonstrates personal and professional courtesy
- Avoids destructive comments and public criticism
- Respects people's work time, personal time and other commitments

- Supports agreed-upon decisions after they are communicated
- Explains reasons for decisions/requirements
- Encourages/accepts constructive criticism
- Gives performance feedback in a timely, objective, honest manner
- Listens attentively
- Solicits different opinions
- Works to build individual's confidence, ability and understanding
- Recognizes others' achievements
- Provides effective coaching and training
- Is available to help when needed
- Shares credit
- Inspires pride in the work team
- Demonstrates commitment to finding solutions

Customer Commitment

Definition
- Meeting the needs of our varied customers comes first

Behaviors
- Is familiar with the spectrum of Exchange Customers
- Has a complete knowledge of personal customers
- Encourages and listens to input from customers
- Considers the Customer's perspective when making decisions
- Clearly demonstrates the importance of all customers

- Never implies that the Exchange is "better" or "above" the customer
- Respects confidentiality when in possession of information about customers
- Demonstrates the flexibility required to best serve customers
- Defines quality in terms of meeting customer needs
- Avoids over-committing to our customers
- Works to meet commitments to customers no matter who made them
- Acts to resolve customer concerns in a timely manner

We are grateful to the New York Stock Exchange for its permission to publish in *Values Added* the complete text of this important Values/Behavior matrix. It provides a special opportunity for managers to build a consensus on values and goals. Then, through collegial discussion of tangible details at all levels in a firm, to identify on-line behaviors which assist or impede the achievement of those values and goals. For further information, call Communications, at (212) 656-3000 or their web site at http://www.nyse.com

I hope my readers will make their own priority list of the top values and goals in *their* specific careers and examine the impact of alternative behaviors in achieving those values. At best the NYSE Values and Behaviors format can be a model for wiser, more responsible decision making in *any* career, *any* industry, *any* life.

Bibliography

Badaracco, Jr., Joseph L., and Richard R. Ellsworth. *Leadership and the Quest for Integrity*. Boston: Harvard Business School Press, 1989.

Bear, Larry Alan, and Rita Maldonado-Bear. *Free Markets, Finance, Ethics and Law*. Englewood Cliffs, New Jersey: Prentice Hall, 1994.

Bronson, Po. *Bombardiers*. New York: Random House, 1995.

Burrough, Bryan, and John Helyar. *Barbarians at the Gate: The Fall of R.J.R. Nabisco*. New York: Harper & Row, 1990.

Casey, John L. *Ethics in the Financial Marketplace*. New York: Scudder, Stevens & Clark, 1988.

Covey, Stephen R. *The 7 Habits of Highly Effective People*. New York: Simon & Schuster, 1990.

Driscoll, Dawn-Marie, W. Michael Hoffman, and Edward S. Petry. *The Ethical Edge: Tales of Organizations That Have Faced Moral Crises*. New York: Master Media, 1995.

Fisher, Roger, Elizabeth Kopelman, and Andres Schneider. *Beyond Machiavelli: Tools For Coping With Conflict*. Cambridge: Harvard University Press, 1994.

Gilligan, Carol. In a Different Voice: Psychological Theory and Women's Development. Cambridge: Harvard University Press, 1982.

Hauerwas, Stanley. *Truthfulness and Tragedy: Further Investigations Into Christian Ethics*. South Bend, Indiana: University of Notre Dame Press, 1986.

Lewis, Michael. *Liar's Poker*. New York: W.W. Norton & Company, Inc., 1989.

Nash, Laura. *Good Intentions Aside: A Manager's Guide to Resolving Ethical Problems*. Boston: Harvard Business School Press, 1990.

Stewart, James B. *Den of Thieves*. New York: Simon & Schuster, 1991.

Tannen, Deborah. *You Just Don't Understand: Women and Men in Conversation*. New York: Ballantine Books, 1990.

Toffler, Barbara Ley. *Tough Choices: Managers Talk Ethics*. New York: John Wylie, 1986.

Train, John. *Famous Financial Fiascos*. New York: Clarkson N. Potter, Inc., 1985.

White, Thomas I., ed. *Business Ethics: A Philosophical Reader*. New York: Macmillan Publishing Co., 1993.

Articles

Badaracco, Jr., Joseph L., and Allen P. Webb. "Business Ethics: A View From the Trenches," *California Management Review* 37, No. 2 (1995): 8-28.

Hu, Henry. "Misunderstood Derivatives: The Causes of Informational Failure and the Promise of Regulatory Incrementalism," *The Yale Law Journal* 102 (1993): 1457-1513.

Moore, Jennifer. "What is Really Unethical About Insider Trading?" *The Journal of Business Ethics* 9, No. 3 (1990):171.

Film

All My Sons. Directed by Arthur Miller. Dramatist Play Service, 1974.

Do The Right Thing. Directed by Spike Lee. MCA Home Video, 1990.

Ethics in America (series of 10 cassettes). Columbia University Series on Media and the Society, available from The Annenberg/CPB Collection at 1-800-LEARNER. Burlington, Vermont, 1989.

Rashomon. Directed by Akira Kurosawa. Janus Collection, 1950.

Wall Street. Directed by Oliver Stone. CBS/Fox Video, 1987.

Index

Original index written by L. Pilar Wyman, Wyman Indexing.

About the Author

John L. Casey is a graduate of Harvard Law School. He practiced law on Wall Street and for 25 years served as a General Partner and Managing Director of Scudder, Stevens & Clark, one of the world's largest investment counsel firms. His writings on business ethics have appeared in *The New York Times, The Bankers Magazine*, and *A Dictionary of Business Ethics*.

About the Editor

Bruce McCandless III is a graduate of the University of Texas School of Law and has practiced securities law in the New York City office of Brown & Wood. He is currently an Assistant Attorney General for the State of Texas.